EARLY AMERICAN CINEMA by Anthony Slide

Above: Broncho Billy Anderson

In the same series,
produced by THE TANTIVY PRESS
and edited by Peter Cowie:

HOLLYWOOD VOLUMES—see back cover

EARLY AMERICAN CINEMA

by ANTHONY SLIDE

(with the assistance of Paul O'Dell)

THE INTERNATIONAL FILM GUIDE SERIES
A. S. BARNES & CO., NEW YORK
A. ZWEMMER LIMITED, LONDON

Acknowledgments

I AM GRATEFUL to the following for the help and assistance that they have given to me: DeWitt Bodeen, John Cunningham, Leslie Flint, T. A. Johnson, Bert Langdon, Liam O'Leary, George Eastman House and the ever-helpful and patient girls in the cataloguing department of the National Film Archive, Patricia Coward, Thelma Schaverien, Elaine Burrows and Elizabeth Thomson.

First hand accounts of the period were given to me by Mrs. Howard Gaye, Helen Gibson, Lillian Gish, Mrs. Thomas Ince, Hal Roach and Blanche Sweet.

Above all, I wish to thank Harold Dunham for generously sharing his immense knowledge of early American film history.

COVER STILLS
Front: Blanche Sweet
Back: John Bunny

FIRST PUBLISHED 1970
Copyright © 1970 by Anthony Slide
Library of Congress Catalog Card No. 71-119639
SBN 302-02059 - 4 (U.K.)
SBN 0-498-07717-9 (U.S.A.)

Printed in the United States of America

Contents

Superior numbers in the text correspond to entries in the Bibliography.

1. The Beginnings: Edison and Lubin

> "It is always rather difficult to make a sweeping statement about the film field, for no one person may ever see it all."—*The New York Dramatic Mirror*, March 31, 1915.

JUST AS IT WAS IMPOSSIBLE in 1915 to make sweeping statements about the cinema, so today it is even more difficult, looking back to that time. It is equally difficult, indeed almost impossible, to compile a complete history of the early years of the American cinema. Too many films have disappeared completely, and even more remain as just titles in trade papers. The sheer number of films produced during the first ten to twelve years of this century daunts any would-be film historian. D. W. Griffith alone directed over five hundred films during his sojourn with American Biograph.

No one can put forward concrete claims for any individual or company as inventor of the close-up, the tracking shot, montage or any other technical or artistic innovation. Even when it is possible to view these early productions, one can never be positive that the print one is seeing is exactly as its maker intended it to be seen; has not been re-edited or in any other way tampered with at some later date. One example is Porter's *The Great Train Robbery,* which according to Terry Ramsaye, was 800 ft. in length, yet the seemingly complete print in the National Film Archive in London is only 586 ft. Could it be that the latter print has been re-edited and more closely cut for re-release later? A glaring example of this type of re-editing is Kalem's 1912 production, *From the Manger to the Cross*, re-edited in 1937 by Brian Hession, who also inserted faked close-up shots. No copy of this film as it was originally shown exists.

The early history of the American cinema is the story of the rise of the film from a peep-show attraction fit only for the lowest of the lower classes to a legitimate entertainment. The middle and upper classes were not to "discover" the movies until D. W. Griffith produced *The Birth of a Nation* in 1915, but that does not mean that the cinema was

Thomas Alva Edison

7

in any way unpopular with a vast number of people before that date. As James Card, curator of the George Eastman House, has said: "Every two months the entire population of the globe was exceeded in number by the total of all who visited the world's silent movies. For unlike the arts of individual expression, the aim of the film has been to reflect in pictures, the universal longings of the multitude."24

*   *   *

For the purposes of this book, the American cinema can be said to have started with Edison. On March 11, 1911, **THOMAS ALVA EDISON** said to the world's press, "When I invented the modern moving picture in the summer of 1889, I sought to do for the eye what the phonograph had done for the ear. The high character of the pictures made by my own company and the other American and foreign manufacturers under my own patents represent a development that has far exceeded my most ambitious hope." Pious words indeed! The success of the film industry had more than exceeded his ambitious hope, for Edison had had little or no faith in moving pictures. Edison had met Eadweard Muybridge in 1888, and considered the idea of combining the phonograph with moving photography. Edison, after the initial idea, took little interest in the project, and one now knows, through the researches of Gordon Hendricks, that credit for the work in which Edison took so much pride in 1911 should in fact go to his assistant, an Englishman, W. K. L. Dickson.

In the grounds of Edison's plant at West Orange, New Jersey, was built the famous "black maria" studio in 1894, and here were produced by Dickson films for peep-show machines, known as kinetoscopes. A typical film was *Bucking Bronco,* produced October 16, 1894 and 643 frames in length. The description is by Gordon Hendricks: "Taken during a visit of members of the Buffalo Bill Wild West Show in West Orange. Lee Martin, of Colorado, is riding 'Sunfish,' while Frank Hammitt stands on the fence and fires a pistol. In the background, press agent Madden waves his stick. The riders were paid $35—including transportation for the horses—for their work."16

On August 18, 1894, Norman C. Raff and Frank R. Gammon formed the Kinetoscope Company to exploit Edison's films in America; abroad they were sold by Maguire and Baucus. These kinetoscope films were first projected on to a screen publicly in a New York theatre on April 23, 1896. The American cinema was born.

The Edison Studios

It is perhaps fitting that in 1900, the year in which this book officially begins, **EDWIN S. PORTER,** whose early films were to be of such importance for the future history of the cinema, joined the Edison Company. Porter was thirty years old when he went to work with Edison; previously he had been a manufacturer of cameras and projectors. Until 1909, when he left the company, Porter was responsible for all production at the Edison studios at 41 East 21st Street.

Porter's first important film was *The Life of an American Fireman.* It is obvious that Porter was familiar with the work of the British filmmakers of this period, and the film bears considerable similarity to J. Williamson's *Fire!* (produced in 1901). For his production, Porter used firemen from four different cities—New York, Newark, Orange and East Orange.

The film opens with a shot of the fire chief asleep at his desk; in a dream he sees his wife and child. The child says her prayers and goes to bed. The fire chief awakens with a premonition of danger. There

9

The sequence of events in THE LIFE OF AN AMERICAN FIREMAN (frame enlargements)

is then a cut to a close-up of Fire Alarm No. 383, a hand (described by George Pratt as "the hand of destiny") enters the frame, opens the door and pulls the lever. In the following scenes, one sees the dormitory of firemen waking up, pulling on their trousers and starting down the pole. Cut to the interior of the fire station with the firemen descending the pole. They harness the horses of the fire wagon and rush off to the right past the camera. In the next shot is the interior of the fire station, with the doors open; the horses and wagons emerge, and again go off right past the camera.

There is then a cut to the scene of the fire, followed by a shot of the interior of the house with a fireman entering the burning room and saving the mother. The fireman is seen descending the ladder and laying the woman on the ground. She regains consciousness and begs the firemen to rescue her child. The previous scenes are then repeated, with the same firemen, and the child replacing the mother as the rescued. The film ends with a shot of the child in her mother's arms.

The whole film is a mere 425 ft. Yet to audiences of the time, there must have been a great deal of excitement in watching the rescue, and even an element of suspense is added as to whether or not the fireman will be in time to rescue the child. The close-up, however, was probably used only in order that the audience might be able to read the words, "Fire Alarm," and I do not believe was intended to serve any dramatic purpose. In recent years, American historians have come to regard this as Porter's most important film. Professor Robert Gessner has written: *"The Life of an American Fireman* is entitled to be considered the single most important improver in the history of the moving image. It is also entitled to a fatherhood claim on *Last Year in Marienbad;* wherein time present and time past are so intricately blended that time becomes meaningless; all that appears to matter is a dream. Like *motion* that has a mysterious psychological *flow*. It is no idle compliment to ask whether Alain Resnais might not be the Edwin Stratton Porter of our day."[13]

In 1903, Porter also produced *Uncle Tom's Cabin,* which seems ludicrous when viewed today with its painted ice floes, and *The Great Train Robbery*. The latter was filmed in the autumn of 1903 and released in December of the same year. The story is too well known to

Edwin S. Porter

warrant description here, and in technique it differs little from *The Life of an American Fireman,* although the tracking shot first of all along and then downwards after the robbery is of interest. The close-up of the bandit (played by George Barnes) firing at the audience is also significant. The original Edison catalogue states: "Realism. A life size picture of Barnes, leader of the outlaw band, taking aim and firing point blank at each individual in the audience. (This effect is gained by foreshortening in making the picture.) The resulting excitement is great. This section of the scene can be used either to begin the subject or to end it, as the operator may choose."

While at Edison, Porter gave D. W. Griffith his first screen role in 1907 in *Rescued from an Eagle's Nest.* (Griffith had come to the studio to sell a scenario of *Tosca.*) Although poor, even in comparison to films made by Porter four years previous, *Rescued from an Eagle's Nest* is a well-told story, and makes nice use of exteriors (shot across the Hudson from New York) cut into studio scenes.

In 1909, Porter left the Edison Company, and formed his own producing company, Rex. In 1913, this company released *Suspense,* which might conceivably have been directed by Porter, although equally possibly it might have been directed by one of its two leading players, Lois Weber and Phillips Smalley. *Suspense* is of particular interest because of one scene. A burglar (Lon Chaney?) is attempting to enter an isolated house; the wife inside alone 'phones her husband for help, and the audience sees the three of them in a triple screen shot—the wife 'phoning, the husband answering and the burglar entering the house. And Abel Gance did not use a triple screen in *Napoleon* until 1925.

Porter later joined Adolph Zukor, and helped to form Famous Players, acting as production manager for the new company. In 1915, he took a company of players, including Pauline Frederick and Thomas Holding, to Rome to direct (in collaboration with Hugh Ford) a film version of Hall Caine's novel, *The Eternal City.* It was Porter's last film. He died in New York City in May 1941.

To return to the Edison Company. Edison by 1910 had a studio at Bronx Park and a stock company of players consisting of Mary Fuller, Laura Sawyer, Rolinda Bainbridge, Bernadine Leist, Mabel Trunelle, Herbert Prior, William Sorelle, William West, Charles Seay, Charles Sutton, Edward Boulder, Marc MacDermott, Miriam Nesbitt and Charles Ogle. The last appeared in a one-reel version of *Frankenstein,* copy-

14

Lon Chaney (?), Phillips Smalley
and Lois Weber in SUSPENSE

righted by Edison in March 1910. The film is of obvious importance as the first major horror film, and I think it worthwhile to detail the plot here.

Frankenstein is a young student, who upon entering college becomes absorbed in the study of life and death. His greatest ambition is to create life. Convinced that he has found the solution, he begins his experiment, only to discover that he has created a monster. The thought of what he has done makes Frankenstein ill, and he returns home, where he is nursed by his father and bride-to-be. He soon recovers his health. Just before his marriage, Frankenstein is seated alone in the library; he glances up at the mirror and sees the reflection of the monster. The monster also sees his own reflection, and is so shocked that he flees. However, the monster is unable to live apart from his creator, and on the wedding night enters Frankenstein's bedroom, attacks both him and his bride and then leaves.

In the final sequence, which according to the Edison Company, "has

LAURA SAWYER

WILLIAM BECHTEL

WILLIAM WEST

MABEL TRUNNELLE

HERBERT PRIOR

CHARLES SEAY

CHARLES OGLE

JOHN R. CUMPSON

MARC McDERMOTT

EDWARD BOULDEN

SCENE FROM

FRANKENSTEIN

Charles Ogle in FRANKENSTEIN

probably never been surpassed in anything shown on the moving picture screen," the monster, so broken down by his attempts to be with his creator, stands before a large mirror and holds out his hands entreatingly. Gradually, the real monster fades away, leaving only his reflection in the mirror. Frankenstein enters the room, and in the mirror sees the monster's reflection and not his own. Only with his love for his bride does the monster image fade, and does Frankenstein see his own image reflected in the mirror once again. In its publicity material for the film, the Edison Company announced, "it will be evident that we have carefully omitted anything which might by any possibility shock any portion of an audience."

17

Other early "horror" films produced during this period include a 1908 *Dr. Jekyll and Mr. Hyde* from the Selig Company, and a 1912 version of the same story from Thanhouser with James Cruze in the leading role.

The Edison Company produced many adaptations from the classics. Among these were: *Alice's Adventures in Wonderland* (1910); *Michael Strogoff* (1910); *The Three Musketeers* (1911, with Sidney Booth as D'Artagnan); *Martin Chuzzlewit* (1912, in three parts, with William West and George Lessey); *The Corsican Brothers* (1912, with George Lessey and Miriam Nesbitt) and *Treasure Island* (1912, with Addison Rothermel and Laura Sawyer). In June 1911, at a time when controversy was raging as to whether an audience would accept close-ups in films, Edison copyrighted *A Comedy of Understanding,* which consisted of close-up shots of nothing but feet.

English cartoonist and writer Harry Furniss had been working for the Edison Company, and it was he who suggested the company might visit England. Thus in the summer of 1912, Ashley Miller (director), H. A. Brederson (cameraman) and two players, Marc MacDermott and Miriam Nesbitt, came on location to England. They shot a number of films at the Hepworth Studios at Walton-on-Thames, usually based on stories by Bannister Merwin. The company returned to New York on October 12, 1912.

Miriam Nesbitt was born and educated in Chicago. She had made her stage *début* on January 20, 1897 in *The Cup of Bethrothal,* and entered films with the Edison Company in 1910. Marc MacDermott was an Englishman, who had gone over to America with Mrs. Patrick Campbell's Company, after several years on the English stage, including portraying Sherlock Holmes at Wyndham's Theatre, London. He was one of the finest character actors with the Edison Company. A critic in 1912 wrote of him: "His face when in repose is striking, but when he is in the grip of some strong emotion, one is fascinated by the play of the features as every muscle responds to the actor's command."

Like most early companies, Edison produced a number of films dealing with social problems. It is amazing how many people believe Griffith to have been the only early producer interested in such problems. Although Edison had once declared that "children are only little animals," in 1912 he produced *Children Who Labour,* based on a story by Ethel Browning. The film is a treatise against child labour, produced

Marc MacDermott in THE PASSER-BY

in co-operation with the U.S. National Child Labour Committee. The film opens with a symbolic scene of toiling masses of children on their way to the mills. A foreigner (John Sturgeon) is unable to obtain work for himself and is forced eventually to send his children out to work for Hanscomb, a wealthy mill owner (Robert Conness). Hanscomb accidentally loses his own daughter on a train journey, and she is discovered by the foreigner, who eventually is forced to send her out also to work at the mill. In the end, the girl is spotted by her father, but refuses to return to him until all the children are freed from their labours. The final title in the film comments, "The condition called 'Child Labour' still exists and demands our attention."

Playing the foreigner's wife in *Children Who Labour* was the delightful Mary Fuller. Miss Fuller joined Edison early in 1911, her first films being *The Try-Out* and *Two Valentines*. She had entered the film industry with Vitagraph in 1907. She left Edison to join Universal Victor in 1914, and retired from the screen two years later. However, she returned briefly to the screen in 1919 to play opposite Lou Tellegen in Lasky's *The Long Trail*.

In 1912, the Edison Company copyrighted *The Passer-by,* based on a story by Marion Brooks, and directed by Oscar Apfel. A passer-by is invited to join a bachelor party, and after a meal is pressed to tell an after-dinner story. The passer-by (Marc MacDermott) stands at the head of the table; the camera tracks in to a close-up of his face, and this is followed by a dissolve to a close-up of the passer-by as a young man at his own bachelor dinner. In the flashback, MacDermott tells of how being jilted by his *fiancée* (Miriam Nesbitt) altered his life, and had made him the penniless man he is now. At the end of the film, it transpires that the dinner was being given by the son of the passer-by's ex-*fiancée* on his wedding eve. MacDermott leaves the party sadly, and once more becomes a passer-by. Apfel's direction is masterly—he also has a small part in the production—and it is strange that he never achieved any real importance as a director.

Photographically interesting is the 1913 *The Man He Might Have Been,* based on a story by James Oppenheim. The boy (Bary O'Moore) is denied further education by his parents, and the film tells in a series of flashback dissolves the man he might have been if he had received such an education. A similar idea had been used in Edison's *An Old Sweetheart of Mine,* copyrighted in October 1911, with Marc MacDermott as an elderly man glancing through an old photograph album, and in a series of flashbacks recalling his youth and childhood sweetheart. Unlike *The Man He Might have Been,* where no hope is offered for the boy, *An Old Sweetheart of Mine* finishes on a happy note, when the childhood sweetheart proves to be the old man's wife.

In August 1915 Edison joined with George Kleine (one of the founders of the Kalem Company) to form a feature film producing and distributing company, Kleine-Edison Feature Film Service. Gladys Hulette was the star of one of the Edison films of that year, *His Chorus Girl Wife*. She was later, of course, to give memorable performances in Henry King's *Tol'able David* and John Ford's *The Iron Horse,* but had commenced her screen career with Edison in 1911 in *Father's Dress Suit* with Leo G. Norman. She followed her success in that film with *The Star Spangled Banner,* playing with Guy Coombs and Charles Ogle. Other Edison feature film players included Shirley Mason and Viola Dana; and the stage actress, Mrs. Fiske, appeared in one of the last Edison feature productions, a seven-reel version of *Vanity Fair* with Richard Tucker and Bigelow Cooper, released in 1916.

The Edison Company made its last film, a six-reel drama *The Unbeliever* directed by Alan Crosland, in 1918. Terry Ramsaye wrote: "It was thirty-one years since Edison's dream in 1887 of 'a machine which should do for the eye what the phonograph did for the ear.' Now the dust is drifted deep on the Edison stage in the abandoned studio in the Bronx and the only sound is the rowdy chatter of sparrows entering through broken panes to build their nests."[25]

On July 6, 1907 *The Moving Picture World* wrote: "His (Edison's) picture machines are lacking in durability, his pictures lack the pulsating life, without which a film is not a hit. In the United States are six or seven large manufacturers, and the first in line are Biograph and Sigmund Lubin. Sigmund Lubin is known for his sensation films which sell like 'hot cakes,' but which demand from the public a large amount of credulity." Some four years later, *Pictures* was to comment: "Lubin may be called the father of the moving picture industry, which as a manufacturer, renter and exhibitor, he did so much to foster in its infancy."

SIGMUND "POP" LUBIN was born in 1851 in Breslau, Germany. He was educated there and in Berlin. At the age of twenty-five, Lubin left Germany and sailed for the United States. He eventually made his home in Philadelphia, and after a variety of occupations including selling jewellery and gold prospecting, Lubin set up in a small business at 237 North 8th Street making eyeglasses. (In Germany, he had been apprenticed to an optician.) Gradually, he developed a knowledge of lenses and an interest in photography, and this culminated in his invention of a projector, which he called a Cineograph. Eventully, he also developed a camera and printer.

Lubin's earliest films, produced in 1897, were of a horse eating hay (15 ft. in length) and a pillow fight between his two daughters. The same year Lubin rented a rooftop for use as a studio, and employed two Pennsylvanian railwaymen to re-enact the Corbett-Fitzsimmons

prize fight which had taken place on March 17, 1897 at Carson City, Nevada. Lubin read out an account of the fight as given in the newspapers, and the railwaymen acted accordingly. As Terry Ramsaye has commented: "This was art—the recreation of an event—and the 'fight by rounds' column was a scenario, but Lubin did not know it."[25] Similarly in 1899 Lubin re-enacted the Jeffries-Fitzsimmons fight, which had taken place at Coney Island on June 9, using two Philadelphia boxers, Billy Leedom and Jack McCormick.

One of the Edison lawsuits over copyright briefly halted Lubin's activities in 1898, when he was forced to return to Germany, but he was soon back in Philadelphia producing an increasing number of pictures, each with the now familiar trade-mark of the Liberty Bell (hung in the Philadelphia State House, and rung at the Declaration of Independence).

In 1904, Edwin S. Porter had directed for Edison *The Great Bank Robbery* (as a sequel to *The Great Train Robbery*); Lubin promptly produced *The Bold Bank Robbery* with a similar story, 600 ft. in length, and selling outright for $66.

At this point, mention must be made briefly of another pioneer, William N. Selig of Chicago, who was producing short films with such lurid titles as *Trapped by Bloodhounds, or, A Lynching at Cripple Creek*. Colonel Selig acquired an entire zoo in 1908, initially so that he might fake a film of Theodore Roosevelt's African safari, but later he found the zoo useful in the production of a series of popular animal films. In 1913 Selig produced the first version of *The Spoilers* with William Farnum, Bessie Eyton and Thomas Santschi.

Lubin built up a first-rate stock company of actors and directors. Harry Myers was the leading director and scriptwriter of the company for five years, and Frank Borzage, who was later to become a leading Hollywood director, started with the Lubin Company as an actor. Ethel Clayton was the most popular of Lubin actresses, appearing in films directed by her husband, Joseph Kaufman (who died in 1919). Born in Champaign (Illinois) in 1890, Ethel Clayton made her film *début* for Lubin in 1912 with *When the Earth Trembled*; she remained with the Company from then on and was the star of one of Lubin's

Sigmund Lubin

Arthur Johnson

last productions, *The Great Divide,* in which she played opposite House Peters in 1916. Miss Clayton died in June 1966.

Popular Lubin acting partnerships were Arthur Johnson and Lottie Briscoe, Harry Myers and Rosemary Theby, and Ormi Hawley and Edwin Carewe. Romaine Fielding was Lubin's leading man. Unhappily, of all the early companies, the films of the Lubin Company appear to be the ones that have not survived.

After her success in Mack Sennett's *Tillie's Punctured Romance,* Marie Dressler travelled to Philadelphia in 1915 to appear in *Tillie's Tomato Surprise.*

In 1912 Lubin purchased the five hundred acre Betzwood Estate on the outskirts of Philadelphia, and here he was able to produce spectacular films such as *The Battle of Gettysburg.* During the course of an interview in 1914, Lubin told something of the empire that he had built up: "I employ over 1,500 people, and my yearly salary list is

Romaine Fielding

well over £150,000. I paid £200,000 for a studio in Berlin, and my studio in Philadelphia cost as much, whilst my beautiful Betzwood, formerly the estate of the late Mr. John Betz, cost me a great deal more. Here we have at our disposal over five hundred acres of the most picturesque land imaginable. There are four complete farms, all crowded with livestock, a large mansion, a deer park, and a two-mile stretch of the beautiful Schuylkill River."

By 1917, Lubin and his studios were to be forgotten. The government's anti-trust laws, and the subsequent law suits, forced him to leave the American motion picture industry that he had done so much to establish. Some of the last films produced at his studios were Billie Reeves comedies; the very last film was titled *The Dawn of Tomorrow*. Lubin continued at optical and photographic work on a small scale until ill health forced him to retire. He died at his home in Ventnor, New Jersey on September 11, 1923.

2. The Vitagraph Company

THE VITAGRAPH COMPANY was certainly the most prolific early production company. It was also the only one of the Patents Group of companies that was to survive the break-up of the Group, and to continue and prosper as an important film producer into the Twenties. As far as audiences attending the cinema before the First World War were concerned, the films of American Biograph directed by Griffith might be artistically superior to any others, but Vitagraph films were by far the most popular.

The list of stars who commenced their careers at Vitagraph is more than impressive. The Vitagraph Company might justifiably be labelled the M-G-M of the early American cinema. Among the stars who made their screen *début* or who rose to fame with Vitagraph were Betty Blythe, Agnes Ayres, Norma Talmadge, Alice Terry (then known as Alice Taft), Rudolph Valentino, Corinne Griffith, Maurice Costello, Rod La Rocque, Anita Stewart, John Bunny, Alice Calhoun, Mr. and Mrs. Sidney Drew, Jean Paige, James Morrison, Adolphe Menjou, Lillian Walker, Clara Kimball Young, Flora Finch, Florence Turner . . . the list is endless.

The Company was founded by two men, **J. STUART BLACKTON** and **ALBERT E. SMITH.** Blackton had been born in Sheffield (England) in 1875, and had arrived in the U.S.A. with his parents at the age of ten. While working as a reporter and cartoonist for the *New York World*, he had been to interview Edison at the West Orange laboratory. Blackton was impressed with Edison's work, and it was arranged that Blackton should be allowed to rent one of the new Edison projecting kinetoscopes. (Whilst at the laboratory Blackton was made the subject of a kinetoscope film, *Blackton, the Evening World Cartoonist.*)

Prior to the delivery of the projector, Blackton had joined forces with two other English emigrants, Albert E. Smith and Ronald Reader. The three formed the International Novelty Company, a decidedly second-rate vaudeville act, which relied heavily on Blackton's capabilities as a cartoonist to entertain the audience. New life was put into the Company with the arrival of the Edison projector. The International Novelty Company became "The American Vitagraph," and the partners

J. Stuart Blackton

presented their first film programme at Tony Pastor's New Fourteenth Street Theatre on March 23, 1896.

The partners, short of money, could not afford to obtain their films from Edison, and so Smith devised a motion picture camera, and Vitagraph were in the film producing business. One of the first subjects that Smith wished to photograph were the Niagara Falls. However, the partners could not afford the train fare to Buffalo, but they learnt of some equally spectacular falls at Passaic, New Jersey. According to Smith, "So to Passaic went Vitagraph, photographed the falls, and presented them as the spray-lashed miracle of Niagara. The film was shown over the entire eastern half of the United States, and not once did we hear anyone challenge their identity."[34] For the next few years, when the real thing was not available, Smith and Blackton were to become very adept at finding a substitute.

In 1897, the Vitagraph Company produced its first fictional subject, *The Burglar on the Roof*, forty-five feet in length. The film was shot at Vitagraph's newly-acquired studios on the roof of the Morse Building at 140 Nassau Street. The single shot item told of the arrest of a burglar by a policeman, who was conveniently loitering on the roof of the building. Blackton played the burglar; Mrs. Olson, the wife of the janitor of the building, was the lady who came to the policeman's assistance, and others involved in the drama were Ernest Oakes, Vitagraph's office boy, and Ronald Reader. According to Smith, the cost of the entire film was three dollars and fifty cents.[34]

On February 15, 1898, the American battleship, "Maine," exploded in Havana harbour. The Spanish occupation of Cuba became a serious political issue, and Vitagraph produced probably the first propaganda film in the history of the cinema showing the tearing of the Spanish flag from a flagstaff, and its replacement with the Stars and Stripes, followed by shots of the funeral of the victims of the "Maine" disaster. Later in the same year, Smith and Blackton went to Cuba and filmed some of the troops involved in the Spanish-American War. What they did not film was the Battle of Santiago Bay. Remembering their earlier success with the false Niagara Falls, Vitagraph produced a fake film of the incident, with cut-out battleships and cigarette smoke to hide any deficiencies in the models.

Albert E. Smith
(courtesy of Jean Paige)

William "Pop" Rock joined the Vitagraph Company in 1899, as an equal partner with Smith and Blackton. He became president of the Company, and remained so until his death on July 27, 1916. It was Rock who sent Smith out to film the Boer War, with the cheering words, "The English will take care of the savages in quick order, and you'll be back in a jiffy son, with some fine pictures."[34]

Smith's pictures of the Boer War were fine indeed, and they ensured Vitagraph's success. The Company continued to produce much actuality material, including the assassination of President McKinley in 1901. A large number of fictional subjects was filmed, as well as a number of commercial films including *How Waterman's Fountain Pens Are Made* and *The History of a Sardine Sandwich*.

J. Stuart Blackton appeared in a series of films for Vitagraph as "Happy Hooligan." The films were based on a cartoon character created by Frederick Burr Opper. Strangely enough, the Edison Company also appear to have made a series of films with the same character as the Library of Congress hold a print of *Happy Hooligan and the Airship*. This film, copyrighted in 1902, and directed by Porter, is thirty-eight feet in length and portrays a man riding a bicycle, suspended beneath a balloon, over the New York skyline. Presumably, it is similar to the series put out by Vitagraph.

Blackton's wife, Pauline Dean, was one of the Company's first regular actresses. Vitagraph was still very much a family concern. However, by 1903, the studio on the roof of the Morse Building was becoming too cramped for Vitagraph's ambitious filming programme, and the Company acquired some land at Flatbush upon which the Vitagraph Studios were built.

About this time Vitagraph produced *Raffles, the Amateur Cracksman*. It was the Company's first one-reel film, starred J. Barney Sherry, and was probably directed by G. M. Anderson. The rights in the story were owned by Theodore Liebler and Co., one of whose stars was Kyrle Bellew. The latter was pestering Liebler and Co. to make a film of his sword fight in another play, in order that he might study technique. In exchange for granting screen rights to Vitagraph, Liebler asked the Company to make the necessary film of Bellew.

In 1907, Vitagraph put under contract its first leading lady, **FLORENCE TURNER**, who was to become known as "The Vitagraph Girl" and also the world's first film star. Florence Turner was a

The Vitagraph Studios at Flatbush

petite girl with a beautiful oval face. Edward Wagenknecht has written: "Nobody in my generation could have had any difficulty in understanding the young Norma Talmadge's enthusiasm for her even before she herself had become a Vitagrapher: 'I would rather have touched the hem of her skirt than to have shaken hands with St. Peter'."[40]

She was born in New York in 1887, and had appeared on the stage from the age of three. While appearing in vaudeville with Charles Bradshaw and Mabel Crawley, she was advised to try for film work because of her ability to make "such awful faces." She joined Vitagraph in the spring of 1907, and remained with the Company for the next six years. Writing in *The Motion Picture Studio* in 1922, Florence Turner said, "Those were the wonderful days when J. Stuart Blackton, Albert Smith, one director, one scenic artist, one property man and myself comprised the Vitagraph stock company, and put our shoulders to the wheel and helped to put the move in movie. We had no cameraman in 1907—Mr. Smith 'took' the scenes and Mr. Blackton the 'stills.' It was a great life!"

31

At left: Florence Turner, at right: Maurice Costello

Playing opposite Florence Turner was usually Maurice Costello, who became the screen's first *matinée* idol; his two daughters Helen and Dolores often played with him at Vitagraph, and later became stars in their own right. At this time actors were expected to act as carpenters scene shifters, etc. when they were not needed on the set, but when Costello joined Vitagraph, he announced grandly, "I am an actor and I will act—but I will not build sets and paint scenery."[25]

Florence Turner proved what a competent actress she was with the variety of the parts that she played at Vitagraph. She protrayed Topsy in *Uncle Tom's Cabin,* Lucie in *A Tale of Two Cities:* Viola in *Twelfth Night* and Juliet in *An Indian Romeo and Juliet.* In 1911, she appeared

HELEN COSTELLO.

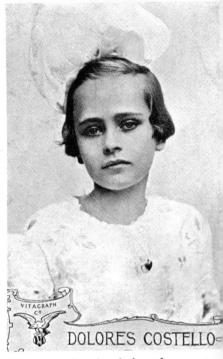

DOLORES COSTELLO

in *Jealousy, the Discarded Favourite,* in which she played the sole character unaided by a single sub-title.

From about 1911 onwards, she appeared always in films directed by Larry Trimble; the latter also was responsible for the series of films featuring Jean, the Vitagraph Dog. Time and time again, Jean was responsible for bringing together young loving couples parted by misunderstandings.

Florence Turner left Vitagraph in the spring of 1913, when she came to England and formed Turner Films Ltd., to produce pictures at Cecil Hepworth's Walton-on-Thames studios. With her came Larry Trimble and Jean. Miss Turner remained in England until 1916 appearing in

Florence Turner as Ben Turpin

some of the best British films of the period, including *East Is East* (with Edith Evans in a small part as Miss Turner's aunt), *Far from the Madding Crowd* and *My Old Dutch.* In 1915 she made *Florence Turner Impersonates Film Favourites,* in which she played a kitchen maid who falls asleep and dreams about her favourite film stars. Miss Turner gave impersonations of Ford Sterling, Mabel Normand, Sarah Bernhardt and Broncho Billy Anderson.

She returned to the U.S.A. in 1916, and appeared in a number of productions including Goldwyn's *Fool's Gold.* By 1920 she was back in England again, where she remained until 1924 when the closure of all British studios in that year found her out of work and penniless. Marion Davies paid her fare back to America, and gave her a small part in one of her pictures. But Florence Turner found it difficult to get work; she can be glimpsed in Buster Keaton's *College,* playing Keaton's mother. *The Motion Picture Classic* in July 1928 painted a pathetic picture of her: "She waits for the studio telephone call that will give her a few days' work. Young-looking and slim, a capable actress, a brilliant pantomimist. . . . What does she ask? Stardom? No. Meaty little parts. Character roles. A chance to come back." During the Thirties she was one of the host of silent stars playing bit parts in M-G-M productions; Florence Turner died in the Motion Picture Country Home in Hollywood on August 28, 1946. Larry Trimble, her director and life-long friend died in February 1954. Edward Wagenknecht said of her, "She was a lovely, idealistic, and unselfish woman, and such she remained, through good fortune and bad, to the end."[40]

Apart from Florence Turner, Vitagraph's other great star of the early days was **JOHN BUNNY**. Bunny's films are something of an enigma to the film historian. They are generally classed as comedies, yet few of them can really be described as comic in the accepted sense of the word. They are far better described as jovial dramas.

John Bunny's screen career was surprisingly short, spanning only five years from 1910 to his death in 1915. He was born in New York, and had a variety of jobs in show business, including nigger minstrel, circus clown and musical comedy actor, before deciding to enter films. In an interview with *Pictures and the Picturegoer* in 1914 he said, "It seemed to me that the cinema—in America at least—was to be the great thing of the future." In these Vitagraph films he was usually partnered by the English-born actress Flora Finch, whose lean angular features and sour manner complemented Bunny's fat features and jolly behaviour, much the same way that Laurel and Hardy complement each other.

The most perfect of Bunny films is *The Troublesome Stepdaughters,* released in 1912. Bunny is a widower, who is posted to the diplomatic service in China, leaving his five, small daughters behind in America. In China he meets and marries Julia Swayne Gordon (a fine dramatic actress, for many years with the Vitagraph stock company). The years pass, and Bunny forgets that by now his children have all grown up. On his arrival home in America, he continues to treat them like children. The girls feel resentful of their new stepmother, and decide to behave like children in order to hurt and upset her. However, they are won over when taken to a dance and introduced to suitable young men by their understanding stepmother. The five girls are played by Norma Talmadge, Edith Storey, Lillian Walker, Dorothy Kelly and Edith Halleran, and also in small parts in this one-reeler are Flora Finch as the housekeeper and Clara Kimball Young as a shop assistant.

In 1912 Bunny came over to England and Ireland, and made a number of films here, such as *Bunny at the Derby* and *Bunny Kisses the Blarney Stone.* He stayed in England during 1913, and played Pickwick in three single reel episodes from *Pickwick Papers,* filmed in Rochester. During 1915, Bunny returned to the stage to appear in a musical comedy, *Bunny in Funnyland.* It was a financial failure, and Bunny used much of his own money to keep the show going. He returned to the Vitagraph studios feeling tired and depressed. Albert Smith recalls, " 'All that is over now, John. A picture will be ready for you Monday morning,' we told him. Monday never came for the man. Poor old John died a few days later."[34] Bunny's partner, Flora Finch, remained in films playing walk-on roles, yet again usually for M-G-M, and she died, completely forgotten, in Hollywood on January 4, 1940.

John Bunny had appeared in a number of three- or four-reel productions (Vitagraph were one of the first companies to regularly produce films of more than two reels in length), including *A Tale of Two Cities* and *Vanity Fair,* in which he played Jos. Sedley. *Vanity Fair* was directed by Charles Kent in 1912, and starred virtually the entire Vitagraph stock company. Seen today, the production is very theatrical, with little use of interior scenes, and it is questionable if English families in the early Nineteenth century had Negro servants. Helen Gardner plays perfectly the shrewd, cunning Becky Sharp. It is easy to see why she should have chosen to play the title role in *Cleopatra,* when she set up in independent production a year after completing *Vanity Fair.* She returned to Vitagraph in 1915, and Edward Wagenknecht writes of a two-reeler made by the Company in that year, *A Still Small Voice,* in which "she played a dumb, half-witted girl who committed murder and then killed herself over the ravages of conscience; I can still see her roaming—as it seemed, endlessly—through the woods, searching for a place to hang herself."[34] Helen Gardner disappeared from screen prominence shortly afterwards, and died in Florida on November 20, 1968.

Helen Gardner was one of the leading players in *The Illumination,*

IN MEMORIAM

JOHN BUNNY
WHO DIED APRIL 26ᵀᴴ 1915.
Regretted by millions all
over the world 𝄞 𝄞 𝄞 𝄞 𝄞

released in 1912, along with Tom Powers, Harry Northrup and Rosemary Theby. *The Illumination* concerns two couples, one Jewish and one Roman, living in Palestine at the time of Christ. One partner from each couple is affected by the teaching of Christ, but the other partners remain unmoved, until they visit the tomb and find that Christ has risen from the dead. (The only item that spoils the film occurs in this scene when an angel in white with large artificial wings appears and announces that "Christ is risen from the dead.") Tom Powers gives a tremendously believable and moving performance of a man who has discovered the meaning of Christ's teaching. Powers later came to England with Florence Turner, and played the title role in Hepworth's *Barnaby Rudge*. Christ is shown only as a light passing across the faces of the onlookers, and the lighting effects are quite marvellous, when one remembers that *The Illumination* was made before the days of pan-

Below: The original opening credits for
THE ILLUMINATION (frame enlargement)

At Right: Tom Powers in THE
ILLUMINATION (frame enlargement)

chromatic film. Others recognisable in the film are Charles Kent, Hal Reid and his son, Wallace Reid (as a centurion).

Also in the same year, Vitagraph released *A Marriage of Convenience,* which is unusual in that it shows a drug addict giving himself a shot. Edith Storey is the heroine in love with James Morrison, but forced to marry the drug addict (an unknown actor) by her parents. Only after the wedding ceremony do the parents discover the man's affliction, and hastily take their daughter away to Europe. The addict is eventually found dead in Central Park, as a result of an overdose of drugs, and the girl is free to marry Morrison, who by this time is serving with the armed forces in the Philippines. Censorship demanded that the addict must atone for his "sin" with his death. It was not until after the death of Wallace Reid (one of Vitagraph's most attractive leading men) as a result of drug addiction, that the public began to feel any sympathy for such people.

NORMA TALMADGE was a superb dramatic actress, whose Twenties films cry out for revival today. Among her features from this period

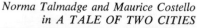

Norma Talmadge and Maurice Costello
in A TALE OF TWO CITIES

Very sincerely your
Norma Talmadge

were *Smilin' Through, Camille* and *The Dove;* she made two talkies, and retired in 1930, after reputedly earning five million dollars. She died at the age of sixty on December 24, 1957. She entered films with the Vitagraph Company in 1910. and made her screen *début* in *The Household Pest.*

Norma's first success came in 1911, when she played Mimi, a seamstress who rides to the guillotine with Sydney Carton (Maurice Costello) in *A Tale of Two Cities;* she is also said to have doubled for Florence Turner who became ill during the making of the film. In 1913 Norma Talmadge was named Vitagraph's most promising newcomer. She appeared in over 250 productions for Vitagraph, occasionally with her sister Constance, before she signed a contract with National Pictures in 1915.

The same year as Norma Talmadge left the Company, Vitagraph released *His Phantom Sweetheart,* directed by Ralph Ince and written by Earle Williams. The latter plays a young man, who falls asleep and dreams of meeting a beautiful woman who invites him to her home, where he is attacked by her husband. Williams awakes, and one of his friends appears to introduce him to the woman that he had just seen in his dreams.

The *Phantom Sweetheart* was played by **ANITA STEWART,** and this film is typical of the dozens in which she co-starred with Earle Williams. Anna M. Stewart was her rightful name, and she acted under that name in many Vitagraph productions until a printer accidentally called her Anita Stewart on a press release, and the name stuck. She was born in Brooklyn on February 7, 1895, and started with the Vitagraph Company as a bit player in 1911; her sister was married to Ralph Ince, and he persuaded her to enter films. (Ralph Ince was, of course, the brother of Thomas H. Ince.)

In 1917, she signed a contract with Louis B. Mayer. Miss Stewart's contract did not expire until January 31, 1918, and so in the spring of 1917, she became conveniently "ill." Vitagraph took the matter to court, which ruled that for all the days that Miss Stewart was "ill," those days would be added on to her Vitagraph contract. This law case is still important today as regards actor-studio contracts. Anita Stewart continued to appear in film until 1928; she died in Beverly Hills on May 4, 1961.

By 1916, many of the companies that had started at the same time

Sincerely Anita Stewart

as Vitagraph were going out of business. Vitagraph, Selig, Essanay and Lubin had joined forces to form VLSE, a distributing organisation; this company was totally acquired by Vitagraph. In the same year, Vitagraph also purchased the Kalem Company.

Film production was changing, and happily Vitagraph managed to change with the times. New stars began to appear, and feature-length production was the order of the day. Edna May, the "Belle of New York," made her only screen appearance in Vitagraph's *Salvation Joan*. Corinne Griffith became a Vitagraph star, playing opposite Earle Williams in films directed by her husband, Webster Campbell. Alice Joyce left Kalem in 1916 to join Vitagraph, starring in films such as *The Vengeance of Durand* (already filmed earlier by Vitagraph with Edith Storey and Earle Williams).

Jean Paige (Mrs. Albert E. Smith) was a beautiful heroine in *Black Beauty*, playing opposite James Morrison. In 1921 she starred with J. Warren Kerrigan in *Captain Blood*.

Rudolph Valentino made his screen *début* at Vitagraph in *My Official Wife*, a film with a Russian background. The technical adviser on the production was an unknown Russian named Leon Trotsky. Also at the Vitagraph studios at the same time, writing scenarios, was a young Irishman named Rex Hitchcock; several years later he was to change his name to Rex Ingram and star Valentino in *The Four Horsemen of the Apocalypse*.

Comedy at the Vitagraph studios was now represented by Larry Semon and Mr. and Mrs. Sidney Drew. The latter were responsible for introducing domestic comedy to the screen. Mrs. Drew was a small-time Vitagraph actress, Jane Morrow, before she met and married Sidney Drew. Their career was all too short; Sidney died in 1919 and Mrs. Drew shortly afterwards.

LARRY SEMON was born in West Point, Mississippi on July 16, 1889, the son of a professional magician, "Zera the Great." In 1916 he visited the Vitagraph studios and became a director there, later turning to comedy acting. Semon appeared in over a hundred comedies for Vitagraph before joining Chadwick Pictures in 1924; for Chadwick he starred in the feature-length *The Wizard of Oz* in 1925. Semon's career was all too short. He contracted tuberculosis, and died in Victorville, California on October 8, 1928.

J. Stuart Blackton was still very active at the Vitagraph studios, and

Larry Semon

in 1917 he directed *Womanhood, the Glory of a Nation*. It was a sequel to his *The Battle Cry of Peace,* one of the earliest of First World War propaganda films, and a production that had created a vogue for war films.

Then in July 1917 Blackton resigned from the Company that he had helped to found twenty-one years earlier, and went into independent production. In 1921 he came to London, where he produced and directed *The Glorious Adventure, The Virgin Queen* and *A Gipsy*

Cavalier. The first two, although critical failures, were both tremendous box-office successes, because of Blackton's use of a famous London beauty, Lady Diana Manners, to play the heroines, and also his use of the prizma colour system. *A Gipsy Cavalier,* which starred Flora Le Breton and Georges Carpentier, has a final rescue sequence every bit as exciting as the final reel of Griffith's *Way Down East.*

Blackton returned to the U.S.A. in 1923, and came back to Vitagraph, becoming one of the Company's supervising producers. He died in Los Angeles on August 13, 1941, after an automobile accident. Blackton was one of the true pioneers of the cinema. He was one of the first producers to realise the cinematic qualities of the works of Shakespeare, and his partner Smith has commented: "Shakespeare can and perhaps by now has thanked Jim Blackton for introducing his comedies and tragedies to films: *Romeo and Juliet, King Lear, Richard the Third, Macbeth, A Midsummer Night's Dream, Twelfth Night.*"[34] He was one of the first of the documentary film-makers, producing in a crude way what would now be described as current affair montages, used so often on television.

The Vitagraph Company passed out of existence in February 1925, when Albert E. Smith sold the entire Company, including its backlog of pictures and its two studios at Flatbush and California (opened in 1911) to Harry Warner of the Warner Brothers. Albert E. Smith writes movingly of this sale in his autobiography: "The studio in Flatbush, the bright and friendly stucco stages with their rows of cottages dozing under the California sun, the hundreds of familiar faces in exchanges around the country, the exhibitors who knew the costs of loyalty and had willingly paid the price of it, the day to day crises: a nervous actor, a weeping actress, a temperamental star—Harry Warner took them under his arm and walked out."[34]

3. The Kalem Company

O F ALL EARLY American films, some of the most beautiful to
look at are those of the Kalem Company. Everything about them
is so natural, so easy on the eye. With the possible exception of the
Griffith films, these are the most perfect in photography, direction,
setting and acting. This quality of naturalness was to a large extent
accidental. The Company had no studios and were forced to shoot
most of their pictures on location, and using local people whenever
possible. Kalem travelled around the world in search of new locations
and new stories.

The Kalem Company's films were the training ground for such
directors as Sidney Olcott, Marshall Neilan, George Melford and James
Horne. Among its leading ladies were Alice Joyce, Anna Q. Nilsson,
Ruth Roland, Miriam Cooper and Mae Marsh (who appeared in two
films for the company in 1912).

The name Kalem is derived from the initials of its three founders:
George Kleine, Samuel Long and Frank Marion. Long and Marion both
came from the Biograph Company, and George Kleine was a Chicago
renter. According to Terry Ramsaye, "Kalem was financed with delightful simplicity. Long owned four hundred dollars worth of partitions

in a loft building where the plant was to be located. Marion contributed six hundred dollars working capital and George Kleine guaranteed the account of the company for the purchase of a Warwick camera from Charles Urban in London."[25] The first film to be made by the company was *The Sleigh Bells,* released early in 1907, and produced in a loft at 131 West 24th Street, New York City. The film was directed by Sidney Olcott and featured Joe and Fred Santley and Robert Vignola.

Vignola, along with George Melford and Gene Gauntier, was one of Kalem's first players. Born in Italy in 1882, Vignola rose from a heavy in Kalem dramas (he was with company at least until 1912) to become a competent director during the Twenties. He died in October 1953. Sidney Olcott spent the last year of his life with Robert Vignola, and it is interesting to note that the part of their careers that they regarded with greatest affection was the years they spent at Kalem. At the time of Olcott's death, Robert Vignola wrote, "We spent many a nostalgic hour recalling our early days on the stage together before we launched into one reel motion pictures, then there were the trips we made filming stories in Ireland, Italy and Palestine. . . ."

The most famous of the early Kalem dramas is undoubtedly *Ben-Hur.* Adapted from Lew Wallace's novel by Gene Gauntier and directed by Sidney Olcott, the film was shot at the Pain's Fireworks Show at Manhattan Beach, with costumes borrowed from the Metropolitan Opera House and chariots raced by the 3rd Brooklyn Battery. Described at the time as "Positively the most superb moving picture spectacle ever made in America," the whole thing seems rather pathetic when viewed today; with a single chariot moving none too quickly along a dirt track, cheered on by half-a-dozen spectators. Unfortunately, the Company had neglected to secure the film rights in the novel and the play with the result that they were soon involved in legal action. Judgement against Kalem was finally delivered in 1912, when the Company was ordered to pay damages amounting to $25,000. The case established that literary rights existed in all filmed works.

The writer responsible for adapting *Ben Hur* for the screen for the first time was Gene Gauntier, leading lady for the Company for many years and generally known as "The Kalem Girl" (Ruth Roland succeeded to the title in 1912). Miss Gauntier was born Genevieve G. Liggett in the 1880s in Texas. She commenced her screen career as an actress with American Biograph, and appeared in several one-reelers

Gene Gauntier

opposite D. W. Griffith. When she joined the Kalem Company late in 1907, she became not only its sole leading lady, but also its assistant director and scriptwriter. Miss Gauntier claimed that she had written practically every one of the five hundred films in which she had appeared, apart from selecting locations, supervising sets, co-directing with Olcott, editing and writing captions and advertising matter. She married another Kalem player, Jack Clarke, during the making of *From the Manger to the Cross;* they were divorced in Kansas City in January 1918. In 1912, with Sidney Olcott, she formed Gene Gauntier Feature Players, which remained in existence until 1915, when Miss Gauntier went over to Universal. She retired from films in 1918. For a time, Miss Gauntier acted as drama and film critic for a Kansas City newspaper, and she published at least one novel, *Sporting Lady,* in 1933. The remainder of her life was spent in travelling. At the time of her death, on December 18, 1966, she was living with her sister, Marguerite (an opera singer) in Cuernavaca, Mexico.

Kalem players were well-known by name; indeed the Company is believed to have been the first to identify its players (although arguments have been put forward in favour of the Imp Company). The Company was also the first to realise the importance of still photographs, and much of the credit for this must go to Bill Wright and George Hollister, Kalem's chief cameraman. New York born, George K. Hollister began his career as a war correspondent and photographer, and covered the Boer War, the Boxer Uprising and the Philippine War. After leaving Kalem, he worked for Thanhouser, Olcott Players and Metro. With the latter, he photographed propaganda films such as *To Hell with the Kaiser,* probably by reason of his having filmed the German Kaiser and his Empress in Berlin in 1911. Hollister's wife, Alice, apart from being a very attractive leading lady for Kalem, was later to gain notoriety in 1914 as the screen's first vamp.

SIDNEY OLCOTT, Kalem's principal director, was of Irish descent, and it was natural that when Frank Marion gave him *carte blanche* to produce films for the Company wherever he liked, Olcott chose Ireland. So it was that in August 1910, Sidney Olcott, with leading lady

Sidney Olcott

Gene Gauntier, Robert Vignola and cameraman George K. Hollister, landed at the Irish port of Queenstown (now Cobh). They stayed for a short while at the Victoria Hotel, Cork, and then moved on to the Glebe Hotel, Killarney. Olcott was not impressed with the town of Killarney, and determined to find a pleasanter spot at which to stay and film. One day, while out touring the countryside in a jaunting car, he stumbled on the village of Beaufort, and decided that it was ideal for his requirements. His efforts to explain what he wanted to do met with some amusement. The people of Beaufort had never seen a motion picture. Olcott asked them if they had seen a magic lantern show. Yes; they knew about magic lantern entertainments. "Well," explained Olcott, "films are like magic lantern slides, but they move." The inhabitants were just as bewildered; however they were willing to help Olcott, and here he filmed *The Lad from Old Ireland*.

The Company also made a number of short films of Irish beauty spots including Blarney Castle, Glengariffe, and of course the lakes of Killarney. Leaving Beaufort, they went on to England where they shot *The Irish Honeymoon,* and then to Germany where they made *The Little Spreewald Maedchen*.

The Lad from Old Ireland was a tremendous success with the Irish immigrants in the U.S.A., so much so that Kalem asked Olcott to return to Ireland in June of the following year with a far larger company. Apart from Olcott, there were Gene Gauntier, Alice Hollister, Alice Mapes, Jack P. McGowan, Jack J. Clarke, Mrs. Clarke, Robert Vignola, Allen Farnham, George Hollister, Arthur Donaldson, Helen Lindroth and Pat O'Malley. The Company stayed at the home of Patrick O'Sullivan in Beaufort. They built a platform in the field behind the O'Sullivan house, and here the interior scenes were filmed. The work of constructing the sets, etc. fell to Allen Farnham, who did not consider himself an actor. The cameraman was again George Hollister.

The first film that the Company made was *Rory O'More,* the story of an Eighteenth century Irish revolutionary hero, set against a background of the lakes and mountains of Killarney. In one scene, Hollister pans his camera across from Rory O'More and his *fiancée* to give the viewer a stunning panorama of the Gap of Dunloe. According to Lewis Jacobs, this film displeased the British authorities, but there seems to be little proof of this.

*Mrs. Clarke, Gene Gauntier, Jack Clarke
and Sidney Olcott in THE COLLEEN BAWN*

The O'Kalems (as the Company laughingly called themselves) and the Beaufort villagers were fast friends. There was no shortage of villagers willing to play small parts in the films. Some villagers even played quite important roles. Miss Annie O'Sullivan (Patrick O'Sullivan's daughter) was one of the female leads in *The Gipsies of Old Ireland*.

Among the films made during the Kalemites' four month stay in Beaufort were *The Fishermen of Ballydavid*, *You Remember Ellen* (based on the poem by Thomas Moore), *Robert Emmet*, *The O'Neil*,

The Kerry Gow and *Conway, The Kerry Dancer.* Three-reel versions of *The Colleen Bawn, Arrah-Na-Pogue* and *The Shaughraun,* taken from the plays of Dion Boucicault, were also made. Only two of these Kalem Irish films are known to be extant, *Rory O'More* and *The Colleen Bawn,* but on the basis of these two pictures, one can see what a very high quality of direction and photography had been reached by Olcott and Hollister. The films made good use of the Irish scenery and of Irish historical relics (one scene in *The Colleen Bawn* featured the actual bed slept in by Daniel O'Connell).

After Sidney Olcott and Gene Gauntier had left Kalem in 1912 and formed the Gene Gauntier Feature Players, they returned to Beaufort the following year to produce a series of films starring Miss Gauntier and Jack Clarke. In 1914 Olcott formed Sid Films, and returned to Beaufort yet again bringing as his leading lady Valentine Grant, who was later to become Mrs. Sidney Olcott. Olcott at this time talked of plans to build a permanent film studio at Beaufort so that he might film there all the year round. Olcott always said that he found it so easy to direct the Irish people; they were natural actors and actresses. Unhappily, the outbreak of the First World War put an end to all his dreams.

As early as the winter of 1908, Kalem had sent a company of players under Sidney Olcott to Jacksonville, Florida; the first film that Olcott produced there being *A Florida Feud.* The film was concerned with the poor whites living outside Jacksonville and made Olcott very unpopular with the civic authorities. The locale was ideal for the production of motion pictures, particularly civil war dramas, as in the near vicinity were civil war vintage locomotives and steamboats.

While Olcott was in Ireland, Kenean Buell took over direction of the Jacksonville Company. Buell was probably responsible for *Tangled Lives,* produced at Jacksonville in 1911 with Carlyle Blackwell, Gene Gauntier and J. P. McGowan. The story is of two children parted in childhood by an Indian attack on their parents' homestead. Years later, they meet, fall in love, and then to their horror discover their relationship to one another. The story is movingly told, and the Florida everglades make a perfect background to the action, the vegetation of the swamps being as tangled as the lives of the central characters.

In the autumn of 1911, the Kalem Irish Company travelled to the Holy Land to produce what was to prove Kalem's most important

*Percy Dyer as the Boy Christ in FROM
THE MANGER TO THE CROSS*

production, the six-reel *From the Manger to the Cross.* Sidney Olcott
was again directing; Gene Gauntier wrote the screenplay and played
the Virgin Mary; Robert Vignola was Judas; Alice Hollister played
Mary Magdalene; Percy Dyer was Christ as a boy and R. Henderson-
Bland played the Christ.

Henderson-Bland was an extraordinary character. An Englishman,
he obviously believed during the production of the film that he was
Christ. He wrote two books about the making of the film, *From the
Manger to the Cross* (published in 1922) and *Actor-Soldier-Poet* (published in 1939). In each he writes as if he had become Christ—chapters

Robert Henderson-Bland as the Christ in
FROM THE MANGER TO THE CROSS

are headed "The Call" and "The Preparation," etc. At one point, he says, "I felt as if I was being enveloped by some strange power and being led gently on."[15]

From the Manger to the Cross tells the story of Christ in a straightforward manner, dealing with the birth, the flight into Egypt, childhood and Crucifixion. Various miracles are shown including the changing of the water into wine, the raising of Lazarus, the man sick of the palsy and the blind Bartimaeus. Two scenes which particularly stand out are the raising of Lazarus, with the white sheeted Lazarus slowly rising from the grave in a most horrific manner and a scene during the childhood of Jesus when the boy Christ is seen carrying a plank of wood from his father's carpenter's shop. The camera pans down to the shadow of the boy, and it almost appears as if the shadow is of Christ on the cross.

The opening sequences up to the Flight into Egypt were filmed in 1911, the remaining sequences in 1912. For the interior shots, a special studio was constructed in Jerusalem (one film magazine of the time put forward the romantic notion that the studio was sited between a nunnery and a monastery). An American, Dr. Schick, was responsible for executing the sets.

Kalem's president Frank Marion in an interview in May 1912 said, "Our aim will be to treat the whole subject with the greatest possible reverence. We shall not offend any doctrine or creed, as we shall rely mainly on the human environment in the development of the story. For the costumes we shall closely follow Tissot, the celebrated painter of Biblical subjects."

The Kalem Company were somewhat concerned that the film might be given an adverse reception from the Church, and so on October 3, 1912, they arranged a special screening of the film at the Queen's Hall London before a thousand members of the clergy. The Company need have no qualms; all who saw it praised it. *The Sunday Express* commented, "so great it seems to me are the possible results of a general presentation of this film that I left the Albert Hall yesterday longing for its exhibition in all the cathedrals, the churches and the chapels in the land, placed, that is, in the atmosphere of reverence to which it absolutely belongs, and used to quicken that imaginative life which is becoming so woefully stunted in an age of triumphant mechanics." Cardinal Bourne said, "a new art has been turned to a noble use with wonderful success."

Kalem produced other films with religious undertones. In 1913, there was *The Atheist* with Tom Moore and Helen Lindroth, the story of an atheist whose faith in God is restored after receiving heavenly help in deciding whether to place love before duty. Duty wins. In 1916 Alice Joyce and Tom Moore appeared in *A Modern Christian.* Nor did Kalem confine themselves entirely to the Christian religion. In 1914, they released *A Passover Miracle,* produced with the assistance of the Bureau of Education in the Jewish Community of New York, and with titles in English and Yiddish.

The Company, while in the Middle East, produced a number of other films. One which unfortunately does not appear to have survived is *Making Photoplays in Egypt*. The most successful of these films was *The Fighting Dervishes of the Desert* with Gene Gauntier and Jack Clarke. The dervishes are seen riding across the horizon line (in a shot reminiscent of the ride of the Clansmen in *The Birth of a Nation*) and the desert is shown as something white and silent keeping its secrets undisturbed by time. Further Kalem productions had such captivating titles as *The Prisoner of the Harem, An Arabian Tragedy* and *Captured by Bedouins*. Particularly moving was *Tragedy of the Desert,* a fatalistic tale of an English doctor who, after discovering his wife's infidelity, joins a nomadic Arab tribe and eventually marries an Arab girl. The years pass by, and his first wife discovers his whereabouts and begs him to return to her. The doctor refuses and escorts her from the Arab encampment, but his Arab wife believes that he is leaving her and commits suicide. Few early films can have had such a tragic ending.

After the production of these films, both Olcott and Gene Gauntier left Kalem. It has always been suggested that their departure had something to do with their making *From the Manger to the Cross* without permission, but this seems unlikely as it is obvious that the heads of the Company in New York were fully aware of what films were being produced in the Middle East.

Sidney Olcott had been born in Toronto on January 20, 1874. He had first entered films as an actor with the American Mutoscope and Biograph Company, with whom he stayed until he joined Kalem at its inception. By the time that Olcott left Kalem he was regarded as one of the cinema's leading directors. He went on to direct Mary Pickford in *Madame Butterfly* and *Poor Little Peppina;* George Arliss in the silent version of *The Green Goddess*; Valentino in *Monsieur Beaucaire* and Pola Negri in *The Charmer*. His last film was *The Claw,* directed in 1927 for Universal, and starring Norman Kerry. After this he came to England to work for British Lion at Elstree, but objected to the moral tone of the films that he was expected to direct. After a lengthy law-suit, which Olcott won, he returned to the U.S.A., but never directed again. He died on December 16, 1949 in Hollywood. It is difficult to appreciate just how much Olcott was responsible for the prosperity of the Kalem Company, but after his departure the

Alice Joyce

Company was to have only another four years of active existence.

When Gene Gauntier left Kalem, her successor as leading lady was Alice Joyce. Born in Kansas City on October 1, 1890, Alice Joyce joined the Company while they were shooting on location at Coytesville New Jersey, and later married another Kalem player, Tom Moore. Her first film for the Company was *The Engineer's Sweetheart*. She was a charming and very gracious leading lady, and her film career spanned the years from 1912 to the Fifties. She died on October 10, 1955.

In the years from 1912 to 1915 many players were introduced to the screen for the first time by Kalem. Billie Rhodes was a young *ingenue* before she discovered her *forte* in comedy. Miriam Cooper appeared in many Kalem railroad dramas, before Griffith invited her to join his company. Carlyle Blackwell, Tom Moore, Guy Coombs, Ed Coxen and Hal Clements were all leading men for the Company. Marin Sais and Ollie Kirby were popular screen partners in Kalem's 1916 serial *The Social Pirates,* and Marin Sais was the leading lady of numerous Westerns during the last few years of Kalem's existence. Paul Hurst, who died so tragically and so utterly forgotten in 1953, played in many Kalem films between 1912 and 1916. His directorial credits for the Company include *The Social Pirates* and several episodes of *The Hazards of Helen.* The popular English actress Ivy Close came over to America to appear in Kalem comedies directed by Fred N. Schierbaum.

With over two hundred films being released annually by the Company, it is difficult to pick out any one as being of especial importance or interest. However, *Trail Through the Hills,* released in 1912, was one of Kalem's better productions, and viewing it today, it is not difficult to see why trade papers at the time described it as "one of the most thrilling and exciting Westerns ever produced."

I have been unable to identify any of the players, or even the director. Indians attack the settler's home, one of the girls escapes to bring help. She leads a rescue party back to the scene of the incident, but one of the men is left behind and attacked by another band of indians. He is flung over a cliff on to a ledge, but his pony is nearby and the animal approaches the cliff, a loosened lariat drops down to the helpless man, and he is able to drag himself to safety. There is a fine sense of timing in the cutting between the man and his only means of help, the pony. The tension is held throughout. Earlier, in a hand-to-hand fight with the indians, the camera is right in the middle of the action, and it is almost as if the camera itself were involved in the fight.

By 1912, Kalem had decided to open a permanent studio on the West Coast, and naturally chose Hollywood as the location for such a studio. Carlyle Blackwell was in charge of operations. An English-

*The unidentified leading lady in TRAIL
THROUGH THE HILLS (frame enlargement)*

man Howard Gaye (who was later to play Robert E. Lee in *The Birth of a Nation* and the Christ in *Intolerance*) joined the Company as a scenario writer, for which he was paid twenty-five dollars a week. In his unpublished autobiography, Gaye describes the Hollywood studio: "The stage of the new Kalem studio was a platform built in the open air about two feet from the ground covering most of the lot. On this the different sets made of 'flats' were erected to represent scenes. Overhead running on wires were adjustable canvas blinds to control the strong sunlight."[9]

To these studios as an actor and director came **MARSHALL NEILAN**. Neilan directed and acted in a series of comedy dramas, usually playing opposite Ruth Roland. Typical of such dramas is *The*

Marshall Neilan

Kidnapped Conductor. Ruth Roland and Marin Sais both lose their jobs on account of lateness because the conductor on the train would not wait for them. To gain their revenge, the girls arrange for the conductor to be kidnapped and ducked in the river. Pleasant little films, not out of the ordinary in production or acting, but they helped to bring fame to both Neilan and Ruth Roland.

Neilan left Kalem to join the American (Flying A) Company in 1912, but he returned to Kalem again in 1914. Here he directed and scripted a series of comedies with Ruth Roland and John E. Brennan. From Flying A he brought over photographer Roy F. Overbaugh and his assistant Victor Fleming (director of *Gone with the Wind*). Neilan also developed a series of comedies with the massive Lloyd Hamilton and the small Bud Duncan. Typical of these "Ham and Bud" comedies was *An Elopement in Rome,* a skit on ancient Rome with Hamilton and Duncan as Fattus and Thinnus. This type of comedy was popular with audiences up to the end of the First World War. Bud Duncan disappeared from the film scene, but Lloyd Hamilton continued to make comedies until the early Thirties.

Neilan left Kalem to go to Lasky as an actor. Later, of course, he became an outstanding feature director, and among his credits are six films for Mary Pickford, *Rebecca of Sunnybrook Farm, A Little Princess, Stella Maris, Amarilly of Clothesline Alley* and *M'liss,* all produced in 1918, and *Daddy Long Legs* made the following year. Neilan died penniless on October 27, 1958 and Mary Pickford is said to have paid for his funeral.

In 1914 Kalem released an extraordinary surrealist film, which one could almost imagine Tod Browning to have directed. The film was

Marshall Neilan in THE KIDNAPPED CONDUCTOR (frame enlargement)

titled *The Fickle Freak,* and unfortunately no print of the film is known to exist. The setting for the story is a circus. The bearded lady is desperately in love with the human pincushion. The latter, however, loves the Circassian lady. The bearded lady shaves off her beard to improve her appearance, but the human pincushion still remains cold. Furthermore, the unfortunate lady loses her job. She next discovers that she has inherited some land, which immediately brings the human pincushion to her feet. But when it is discovered that the piece of real estate is only a plot in the local cemetery, the human pincushion returns to his former love. Mad with jealousy, the bearded lady tries to stab the fickle freak. Unfortunately, she had overlooked the fact that he is a human pincushion, and her efforts are in vain. A more tasteless comedy it would be hard to imagine!

The Kalem Company resisted all attempts at feature production by their own directors for some strange reason, yet the owners of Kalem did not hesitate to invest in the features of other companies. When W. W. Hodkinson founded his own company (later to become Paramount), both Long and Marion invested heavily in shares. As has been mentioned previously, George Kleine joined Edison in feature film production, and was also responsible for backing the 1913 *Quo Vadis?.*

Kalem's lack of interest in feature film production seems even more extraordinary when one considers that when the Company was sold to Vitagraph in 1916 for a reputed hundred thousand dollars, one of the most valuable assets of the Company was the negative of *From the Manger to the Cross,* its only feature-length production.

A fitting epitaph for the Kalem Company appeared in *The Bioscope* of June 27, 1912: "The Kalem Company are quite unique. They are strolling players, whose stage is the whole world, and whose source of inspiration is the whole world's history. They are realising the possibilities of the Picture Play in one of its fullest and most unlimited aspects as a form of drama which is not confined within the four walls of a theatre, and which is not reliant upon artificial contrivances for its scenery, but which may present a picture of life actually and exactly as it is."

4. The Essanay Company

FOR COMEDY and Westerns, the Essanay Company is deserving of an important place in the history of the early American cinema. Chaplin produced some of the best of his early comedies at Essanay, and here also Max Linder was able to bring his comic art before a wider public. Through Broncho Billy Anderson's work at Essanay, the Western film was established as a popular form of screen entertainment.

The Essanay Company of Chicago was founded in February 1907 by **GEORGE K. SPOOR** and **G. M. ANDERSON**. The title, Essanay, was devised by putting together the surname initials of the founders of the Company, S and A. For their trademark Spoor and Anderson chose to borrow the Indian head from the American cent piece.

George K. Spoor was the proprietor of the National Film Renting Company in Chicago when Anderson approached him with the idea of forming a production company. G. M. Anderson—or to give him his correct name Max Aronson—had entered films with Edison and *The Great Train Robbery*. He had gained a part in the Porter production by claiming to be an expert horseman, "I was born on a horse and raised in Missouri," he claimed. In actual fact, Anderson had never ridden a horse in his life, nor had he been a cowboy. The nearest that he had got to the Wild West was posing as a cowboy for a magazine cover.

Anderson moved from the Edison to the Vitagraph Company, acting in and directing a number of one-reelers, but he desperately wanted to produce Westerns, and Vitagraph would not consider such stories. So Anderson moved on to Selig. However, he became dissatisfied with the Western productions that he was involved in at Selig; they were little more than travelogues. So it was that he decided to join forces with Spoor, and make exactly the type of films that *he* wanted to produce.

In 1908 at Golden, Colorado Anderson began filming *Broncho Billy and the Baby* (based on a story by Peter B. Kyne). It was to be the first of 376 Broncho Billy Anderson Westerns, all one or two reels in length. Anderson realised that if his Westerns were to be a success, he must have the same central character in each production;

G. M. Anderson in BRONCO BILLY AND THE BABY (1914)

a character with whom the audience could sympathise. It did not matter if Broncho Billy was sheriff or villain, so long as the films featured Anderson they were a success.

Broncho Billy Anderson became the first great Western film star. Later W. S. Hart and Tom Mix were to usurp his popularity, but virtually until 1915 Anderson was supreme. In most of his films the leading lady was either Marguerite Clayton or Evelyn Selbie, and the other man was usually Arthur Mackely.

Anderson's Western stock company would travel in a special train, fitted with a laboratory so that the film could be developed as soon as it was exposed. The company would travel from Chicago to Denver City, and then on to Colorado, New Mexico and Wyoming, stopping whenever a suitable location was found. The reason for such attention to detail was explained by Essanay: "We do not believe it possible to faithfully reproduce Western pictures—call them cowboy pictures if you will—without going right out into the districts which the film is supposed to portray. The people of the United States, in particular, insist upon Western films being really Western films, and that the Essanay Company have been successful in their efforts is proved by the fact that their Western films are accepted and approved by Western audiences, who would be the last people in the world to accept substitutions artificially staged in the East."[41]

By 1915, Anderson had more or less retired from active film-making, and concentrated on the business side of motion picture production. Broncho Billy now lives in retirement in California. Asked what he had been doing since his retirement he replied simply, "Just driftin' along with the breeze."

Anderson had, shortly after joining Essanay, appeared in his own production, *The Best Man Wins,* 895 feet in length. He so proved that a film of over half a reel in length was quite acceptable to cinema audiences. In 1909 Essanay produced *Shanghaied* and *Maud Müller,* each one thousand feet in length. They were two of the first American one-reel productions.

The word "photoplay" was first used to describe a motion picture in the autumn of 1910 by the Essanay Company. Essanay had conducted a newspaper contest "with the object of finding a suitable synonym which would not only be descriptive, but would sum up in one word the spectacular entertainment afforded by picture theatres." The winning word "photoplay" was contributed by a Mr. Edgar Strakosch. The house organ of the Company was promptly named *The Photoplay Review.*

Back to the Old Farm, a one-reeler produced by Essanay in 1911 for the International Harvester Company of America, was the first acted film to be used for industrial advertising purposes. It was shot on location at Wayne, Illinois and at Essanay's Chicago studios. The story was written by E. L. Barker and the leading lady was Beverly Bayne. The simple story can be told by quoting the actual captions used in the film:

1. George receives an invitation to spend his vacation on the old farm.
2. That night he dreams of the drudgery of farming as he knew it.
3. He recalls the labor of picking up the grain cut by the early reaper.
4. Of the nuisance of unhitching, feeding and watering a team of horses.

5. On his return he surprises his boyhood sweetheart, Beverly Bayne.
6. She shows him how new machinery has taken the drudgery from farming.
7. A modern gas engine generates current to separate milk churn butter.
8. An auto wagon, early International truck, hauls passengers and produce.
9. Childhood sweethearts, they elope in the farm's modern carriage.
10. The mailman's International truck brings news of the happy finale!

Here was more than an advertising gimmick. The cinema at last was being used to inform—to tell the farming communities of modern agricultural machinery.

Beverly Bayne, the star of *Back to the Farm,* formed a romantic film partnership at Essanay with Francis X. Bushman; indeed for a time they were husband and wife both on screen and off. Miss Bayne was attending school at Chicago, when she was offered a screen role at Essanay by director, Harry McRae Webster. The film, *Loan Shark,* was to be the first of some five hundred films in which she appeared. Of her performance in *Romeo and Juliet,* E. H. Sothern wrote, "the loveliest Juliet of the silent movies . . . young and beautiful." She left Essanay to appear in comedy sketches on the Keith-Orpheum circuit, and appeared regularly on the stage until recent years. She now lives in retirement in Scottsdale, Arizona.

FRANCIS XAVIER BUSHMAN made his screen *début* with the Essanay Company in 1911; in the same year he had been named America's "Most Handsome Man" in a competition sponsored by *The Ladies World.* Previous to his screen career, Bushman had worked, amongst other things, as a sculptor's model and trick cyclist. He remained with Essanay until 1915, appearing in literally hundreds of films. With Beverly Bayne, he joined the newly-formed Metro Company, and it was with this company that they made *Romeo and Juliet* together.

At the World's Fair at San Diego in 1915, Bushman was given the title "King of the Movies." The previous year he had been voted leading world film star, again by *The Ladies World.* His screen appearances after 1916 became fewer, but his career received a boost

*Francis X. Bushman and Beverly Bayne featured
on publicity material for ROMEO AND JULIET*

when in 1924 he was cast by M-G-M as Messala in *Ben Hur*. Sadly, following his success in *Ben-Hur,* Bushman was blacklisted for an unknown reason by Louis B. Mayer, and retired from films until the mid-Forties. From then until the date of his death on August 25, 1966, Bushman continued to make brief appearances in films.

After Bushman had left Essanay, **HENRY B. WALTHALL** became the Company's new leading man. One of his most successful films for Essanay was the three-reeler *Temper,* written by H. S. Sheldon and co-starring Ruth Stonehouse and Wanda Howard. The story concerned a son who inherits the violent temper of his father, whom he later kills to prevent his attacking the mother. At the son's trial the jury brings in a verdict of justifiable homicide. A contemporary critic wrote of Walthall's performance: "He brings out the feelings with an intensity that makes it real."

Walthall co-starred with Edna Mayo in the fifteen-episode, Essanay

Henry B. Walthall

serial *The Strange Case of Mary Page*. All of the gowns that Miss Mayo wore in this serial were specially created for her by Lucile (Lady Duff Gordon), one of the most important and celebrated fashion designers of her day. This was probably the first time that anyone from the world of fashion had given their name and seal of approval to the cinema. Lady Duff Gordon was also responsible for Edna Mayo's costumes in the 1916 Gold Medal feature, *The Misleading Lady,* in which Walthall was again the co-star.

The Essanay Company was particularly successful in the comedy field. Apart from Chaplin, who is dealt with later in this chapter, Essanay had many other popular comedians under contract.

One of the Company's first comedy stars was Alkali Ike, played by Augustus Carney. A typical Alkali Ike success was *Alkali Ike and the Devil,* released in 1912. Ike and his girl friend are invited to a fancy dress ball. Ike decides to go as the Devil, but his girl friend is prevented from accompanying him by her father. Needless to say, *en route* to the ball Ike is mistaken for the Devil with disastrous results, but his disguise helps him to put to flight a gang of thieves who are attacking his girl friend's father. The film ends with Ike setting out for the dance again, this time in the company of his girl friend.

Another popular early comedy series at Essanay were the Snakeville Comedies with The Joyous Trio; Margaret Joslin as Sophie Clutts, Harry Todd as Mustang Pete, and Victor Potel as Slippery Slim. Also appearing in Snakeville Comedies was a comedian who was later to become a star in his own right—Ben Turpin.

MAX LINDER, the great French comedian, made his American *début* with Essanay in 1917. He signed a contract with Spoor to appear in a two-reel comedy every month, supported by an American cast and with an American director. Linder's first American production, *Max Comes Across,* was released on February 6, 1917. It was not well received by either critics or public. As Terry Ramsaye unkindly wrote, "Max came across, but he did not go over."[25] Linder made two further films for Essanay, *Max Wants a Divorce* and *Max and His Taxi.* The latter was undoubtedly the best of the three films, and was quite favourably received. In it, Max used the gag of a drunken man harnessing a horse the wrong way round; a comedy routine that Chaplin was later to borrow and use in *City Lights.*

Linder quarreled with Spoor, and his $5,000 a week contract was cancelled. Essanay's publicity claimed that Linder was ill, and feeling the after-effects of wounds he had received fighting in the First World War.

Obviously Max Linder believed that he could make a success of producing films in America. For in 1919 he came to Hollywood, and formed his own production company, releasing through Robertson-Cole. He produced three films here, all directed and scripted by himself; they were *Seven Years' Bad Luck* (an unfortunate title), *Be My Wife* and *The Three Must-Get-Theres* (a skit on Fairbanks's *The*

71

Three Musketeers). All three were without doubt brilliant comedies, but they were not what the public at that time wanted. Linder left the U.S.A. in the autumn of 1922, a bitter man. On October 30, 1925 in a Paris hotel room with his attractive young wife, Linder committed suicide. As a mark of respect Chaplin closed his studios for the day.

The comedian who is obviously the best remembered of the Essanay Company, and the one who was to make millionaires of both Spoor and Anderson is, of course, **CHARLIE CHAPLIN**. The early life of Chaplin is too well known to require reiteration here. Chaplin had been working for Mack Sennett's Keystone Company for exactly a year, when early in 1915 his contract came up for renewal. Chaplin demanded a new contract, guaranteeing him $750 a week. Sennett would not meet this demand, and so Chaplin turned his attentions to Essanay, at the same time making a new demand of $1,250 a week. This demand was met, and on January 2, 1915, the Company announced that Chaplin was now an Essanay star.

Chaplin's first film for Essanay, appropriately titled *His New Job,* was produced at the Company's Chicago studios. His cameraman was Rollie Totheroh, who was to remain with Chaplin until *Monsieur Verdoux* in 1947. Other Chaplin regulars making their first appearances with him in that film were Ben Turpin and Leo White. Playing the role of a secretary was an Essanay extra named Gloria Swanson.

Moving Picture World described *His New Job as* "the funniest comedy ever filmed." In a publicity release Essanay explained how Chaplin worked: "Mr. Chaplin produced the play without any scenario whatever, although he had carefully thought out the outlines of his plot beforehand. Most of the incidents and practically all of the little mirth producing tricks were extemporaneous, however, Mr. Chaplin originating them as the camera clicked out the film."

Chaplin disliked the cold Chicago climate—he had been used to filming in California—and for all his subsequent Essanay productions he returned to California. The next Chaplin comedy, *A Night Out,* released February 15, 1915, introduced a new leading lady in Edna Purviance.

Miss Purviance was born in 1894 in Reno, Nevada, and had been a typist before entering films. She was a perfect partner for Chaplin

Max Linder in THE THREE MUST-GET-THERES

Ben Turpin and Charlie Chaplin in HIS NEW JOB

with her classical blonde beauty, and for the next nine years she was to appear in thirty-five of his productions. In 1923 she proved what a capable dramatic actress she could have been when Chaplin directed her in *A Woman of Paris.* Miss Purviance died on January 13, 1958.

Chaplin made three further films, *The Champion, In the Park* and *The Jitney Elopement,* until the first so-called "Chaplin classic" *The Tramp* was released on April 11, 1915. As Theodore Huff has pointed out *The Tramp* remains one of Chaplin's most important productions, because it is the first film in which he introduces a note of pathos.[18] It is perhaps the first comedy film with a sad ending. Chaplin, the Tramp, has saved a girl (Edna Purviance) from a band of robbers, and the girl's father rewards him with a job on his farm. The robbers

Charlie Chaplin and Edna Purviance in THE TRAMP

next attempt to rob the father, but Chaplin again comes to the rescue, but is shot in the leg. He is nursed back to health by the girl and everything seems perfect until the girl's *fiancé* (Lloyd Bacon) returns home. Sadly, Chaplin writes a farewell note, ties up his bundle of belongings and leaves. The final shot shows him walking down the road towards the horizon, giving a philosophic shrug as the scene irises out. That final shot was almost to become Chaplin's trademark.

Chaplin appeared in fifteen films for Essanay: *His New Job, A Night Out, The Champion, In the Park, The Jitney Elopement, The Tramp, By the Sea, Work, A Woman, The Bank, Shanghaied, A Night in the Show, Chaplin's Burlesque on Carmen, Police* and *Triple Trouble.* Each of them he used to perfect the character of the tramp,

AUGUSTUS CARNEY ("ALKALI" IKE)

WILLIAM BAILEY

CHAS. HITCHCOCK

RUTH STONEHOUSE

RICHARD BOLGER

HARRY NORTON

EVELYN SELBIE

VIRGINIA AMES

ESSANAY

CLARA SMITH

MARGARET JOSLYN

RICHARD C. TRAVERS

MINOR WATSON

RUTH HENNESSY

LOUIS THEUER

ELEANOR KAHN

THOMAS SHIRLEY

MARGARET MYLIN

DORIS MITCHELL

JOHN DEVEREAUX

JUANITA DALMOREZ

BRYANT WASHBURN

HARRY TODD

"BILLY" MASON

LILLIAN DREW

FRANK DAYTON

FRANCIS X. BUSHMAN

LAYERS

BESSIE SANKEY

THOMAS COMMERFORD

FRANK OWENS

WALLACE BEERY

DOLORES CASSINELLI

E. H. CALVERT

HELEN DUNBAR

TRUE BOARDMAN

JULES FERRAR

GERTRUDE FORBES

MAY TAYLOR

GERTRUDE SCOTT

CHAS. STINE

HAZEL APPLEGATE

FRED CHURCH

ANNIE EDNEY

MARGARET BILG

BEVERLY BAYNE

and he introduced new elements such as irony and satire. In these films the pace began to slow down, the old Keystone style of furious pantomime and slapstick was put to one side, and a more subtle form of humour took its place. It is impossible to single out any particular comedy from this period as being better than any other. Each film was an experiment by Chaplin in the art of screen comedy. Theodore Huff describes the Essanay films as being "a transition from the Keystone charades to the polished Mutual series."[18]

Broncho Billy Anderson and Chaplin were close friends at Essanay, and Anderson made a guest appearance as a spectator in *The Champion*. Similarly Chaplin appeared in a drama titled *His Regeneration,* which featured Ethel Clayton and Anderson.

At the end of 1915 Chaplin's contract with Essanay came up for renewal. Just as a year previous Sennett had had to fight to try and keep his star, now Essanay had to fight. Spoor offered him a profit-sharing contract, which guaranteed Chaplin a minimum of $500,000. Chaplin refused the offer, and sent his brother Sydney to New York to negotiate with other film companies. Eventually, on February 26, 1916, Chaplin signed with the Mutual Company. His salary was to be $10,000 a week, plus a bonus of $150,000. The passing of Chaplin was to mark the beginning of the end for Essanay.

There is a curious link between Essanay and Chaplin in that Jackie Coogan, who was to gain screen immortality in Chaplin's 1921 success *The Kid,* made his screen *début* with Essanay in the 1917 five-reeler *Skinner's Boy,* featuring Bryant Washburn. Essanay had a number of child stars under contract, including Little Mary McAllister, a six year old, who appeared in a series of six two-reel dramas described as "the embodiment of childish *naïveté.*"

Two other six year olds, Ida and Ella Mackenzie were known as The Essanay Twins. Typical of their films was *The Little Prospector,* released in 1916. The twins play the two naughty children of an un-successful gold miner and his wife. Their tricks with father's dynamite result in a rich vein of gold being uncovered, and so bring wealth to their parents.

After Chaplin's departure from Essanay, Anderson sold his share of the Company to Spoor. "It was the beginning of the end of the greatness of Essanay,"[25] writes Terry Ramsaye.

By 1917 only four of the original member companies of the Patents

THE RENDEZVOUS

"COME on, my dear; we won't have many more nights together before I go to the Front. Where shall we go? Somewhere where it's cool, quiet, and restful. No, not to a cafe—cakes aren't in my line now I've thrown aside fancy socks and pretty ties, and have settled down to training. The Cinema, that's a good idea. Hope there's something I can tell the other boys about—something to make them laugh. We all fight better when we're cheerful. Here's the Cinema, and, yes, thank goodness, they've got a jolly **"Snakeville" Comedy**; that's ripping.

"We'll come again next week and see what CHARLIE CHAPLIN'S latest 'ESSANAY' is like. I hear he's better than ever.

"Oh! do stop laughing.

"That Indian's head takes a lot of beating as a trade-mark, eh! Mary?"

ESSANAY FILM MANUFACTURING CO.,
148, Charing Cross Road,
London, W.C.

Group remained—Kleine, Edison, Selig and Essanay (Vitagraph had by now gone its own successful independent way). Spoor united these four companies into a new organisation, K.E.S.E., which was to have a short life. At the same time Spoor joined forces with Edison to form Perfection Pictures, releasing through Essanay. This arrangement had a short life, and Spoor released his last productions through Triangle. Among these features, incidentally, was a version of *Ruggles of Red Gap* starring Taylor Holmes (father of Thirties star Phillips Holmes).

Spoor did not cease his film activities with the demise of Essanay. In 1925 he screened 3-D films in Chicago, and renounced them as "impractical and too expensive." Spoor also worked with P. John Berggren on the development of a wide-screen process known as Natural Vision. The invention used a film 70mm wide and was shown on a screen seventy feet wide by thirty-four feet high. In 1930 RKO released one feature *Danger Lights* using the new process. Spoor has always claimed that the Motion Picture Producers Association ("most of whom I put into the picture business") persuaded RKO to discontinue use of the process. Spoor died at the age of eighty-one November 24, 1953. In an obituary notice *Variety* stated, "He made Chicago the film capital of the world."

It is true to say that had it not been for the Chaplin productions Essanay would be completely forgotten today.

5. The Independents

TO UNDERSTAND the important role that the independent film producers, and in particular Carl Laemmle and William Fox, played in the early history of the American cinema, it is necessary to know something of the activities of the Motion Picture Patents Company.

Founded in 1908, the Motion Picture Patents Company was a powerful group of pioneer producers and distributors, consisting of Edison, Vitagraph, Kalem, Lubin, Selig, Essanay, Pathé Frères, Méliès and French Gaumont. Each of these companies handed over to the Patents Company all its patent claims, and agreed to pay Edison a royalty fee for the right to produce and distribute films in the United States. In other words, each company recognised Edison as the inventor of the motion picture, and agreed that it could only produce films with his approval.

General Film was established by the Company in 1909, and it was responsible for the distribution of the Company's films to *licensed* theatre exhibitors only. Non-licensed exhibitors were refused films. Thus, the Motion Picture Patents Company had to all intents and purposes monopolised the American film industry. No film could be legally produced, distributed or exhibited by any person or company not a member of the Patents Company group.

Many pirate producing and distributing companies sprang up, which refused to join, or were not invited to join, the Motion Picture Patents Company. These producers were forced to make films as far away as possible from the detectives employed to track down and harass independent film-makers by the New York based Patents Company. Thus California, with its ideal climate for open-air filming and its great distance from New York, was gradually to become the centre of the American film industry.

Typical of the small independent companies was American Flying A; as Terry Ramsaye said, "the Flying A learned to fly, eluding the heated pursuit of the Patents Company."[25] The company was founded in 1910 by John R. Freuler (later President of the Mutual releasing organisation) and Samuel Hutchinson, and was to have a surprisingly long life for a company which is now completely forgotten.

American Flying A started by shooting Westerns at its open-air studios at Niles, California. In its first publicity statement on its activities, issued in 1911, the Company said: "There is no artificial lighting system in a studio that can approach the perfection of sunlight. There is no scenic artist who has ever been born who could originate and paint scenery that will anywhere equal the stupendous scenic beauties of the Western country. We propose to instil into Flying A Cowboy films the spirit of the West as it really is, the atmosphere of the West as it really was, and the romance of Western life as everybody, even the Westerners themselves, fondly imagine it had ought to be."

Many artists were lured away from the Essanay Company, including

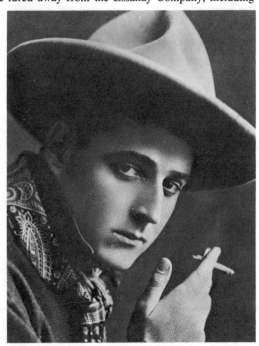

J. Warren Kerrigan

director Allan Dwan, leading lady Pauline Bush (Mrs. Allan Dwan) and leading man J. Warren Kerrigan. Kerrigan, who died on June 9, 1947 at the age of sixty-seven, was a rugged outdoor hero who could not really be considered handsome by present day standards of beauty. He had entered the film industry in 1910; his first film being *A Voice from the Fireplace*. He is best remembered for his performance as the hero of James Cruze's 1923 version of *The Covered Wagon*. Kerrigan retired from the screen shortly after completing the film.

By 1914 American Flying A had a studio in Chicago, and apart from Westerns were producing sentimental dramas such as *Motherhood,* with Katie Fischer as cupid, and described as "the acme of allegorical art." The same year the Company also produced *The Cricket on the Hearth,* adapted from Dickens, with Sydney Ayers as Caleb Plummer and Vivian Rich as Dot. *Moving Picture World* commented, "the atmosphere is decidedly English, and the titles are of the old English style which add a novelty touch to the production. The photographic quality is par excellence and a credit to the American." 1914 also saw the creation of a new associated company, American Beauty Films, which produced a series of pictures starring Marguerite Fischer (sister of Katie) under the direction of her husband Harry Pollard.

Damaged Goods by Eugène Brieux, with its theme of the dangers of venereal disease, had created a sensation when it was staged in New York in 1913 with Richard Bennett (father of Constance and Joan) in the lead. In 1915, American Flying A invited Bennett to re-create his role for the motion picture camera. The film cost $40,000 to produce, and according to Terry Ramsaye, "the promotional opening at a Broadway theatre included a lecture by Dr. Carleton Simon on civilization by syphilization, it brought in a gross of $600,000."[25] The film was re-made in 1919 in Great Britain by Bertie Samuelson.

By 1916, American Flying A, releasing through Mutual, had nine directors and nine associated companies, together with a new studio at Santa Barbara. Some of these associated companies were American Distinctive Creations, Clipper, Mustang, Vogue (making comedies) and Signal. The latter had captured J. P. McGowan and Helen Holmes from Kalem, and starred them in the railroad series *The Girl and the Game*. Signal had its studio built right on a railway line and even possessed its own station.

Clipper produced three-reel sociological dramas, "based for the most part on the works of authors of repute," starring May Allison and Harold Lockwood. This was a very popular screen partnership which lasted until Lockwood's death in 1918. The first Clipper feature was *The Great Question*. Mustang, as its title suggests, turned out Westerns, usually written by C. E. Van Loan, and featuring Art (or Arthur) Acord, Anna Little, Jack Richardson and E. Forrest Taylor. Mustang Westerns were described as "clean, healthy and full-blooded." Features were produced by American Distinctive Creations, and among the first of these were *The Quest* with Marguerite Fischer and *The Lure of the Mask* with Harold Lockwood.

American Flying A remained in existence until the Twenties, and even in its last years had stars of the magnitude of Mary Miles Minter (she appeared in 1918 under the direction of Edward Sloman in *The Ghost of Rosie Taylor*) under contract.

In 1906 Sol Brill, a New York cloth sponger, heard that a penny arcade and picture show was for sale. He told his friend and fellow cloth sponger, William Fox, about this, and together they raised the thousand pounds necessary to purchase the concern. Brill later withdrew from the business. "Fox stayed. He was due to conduct a spectacular war, all of his own, against the rising patents Kings in the next few years."[25]

WILLIAM FOX had been born in Hungary of German parentage in 1879. He was still an infant when his parents emigrated to the U.S.A. In the years to come he was to christen himself with the nickname of "The Fox" and did not resent in the slightest being referred to in that way.

From one small nickelodeon business, William Fox expanded his business activities until by 1910 he had ownership of a large group of theatres in New York. His Company was called the Greater New York Film Rental Company. At the same time, the Patents Company were busily engaged in purchasing exchanges (i.e. small film distribution centres) and theatres. By October 1910, of 9,400 theatres in the U.S.A., 5,281 were under the control of the Patents Company. Those that would not sell out to the Patents Company were refused films; few people were willing to fight the mighty Patents Company led by J. J. Kennedy (the then head of the Kennedy family).

William Fox

Only one New York exchangeman refused to give in to the Patents Company—he was William Fox. Fox, with financial backing from wealthy Tim Sullivan and the legal advice of attorney Gustavus A. Rogers, embarked on an injunction suit against the Patents Company and the General Film Company in the Federal courts. At the same time, Rogers met representatives of the Attorney General and President Wilson, and stressed to them that the Patents Company and the General Film Company were engaged in "an unlawful conspiracy in restraint of trade."

A government dissolution suit against the Patents Company began on January 15, 1913. H. N. Marvin from American Biograph and William Pelzer of Edison were the first witnesses. The case dragged on for years until the Patents Company was eventually ordered to "discontinue unlawful acts." The final court case against the Company was in 1917, when the United States Supreme Court held that the Patents Company could not enforce the use of licensed film on patented projectors in cinemas. J. J. Kennedy held the last meeting of the stockholders of the General Film Company in June 1919.

Long before that time, however, both the Patents Company and the General Film Company were of little importance. The final court decisions mattered not at all. The Patents Company had exhausted itself in petty squabbling, expensive legal actions and above all in its failure to realise that the future of the film industry rested not with one-, two-, and three-reel pictures, but with feature-length production.

In the summer of 1913, William Fox decided to embark on film production and distribution, and announced the formation of Box Office Attractions to purchase films for distribution. The first films that the new company distributed were purchased from the Balboa Company, which although fairly small was important enough to have stars such as Ruth Roland and Henry B. Walthall under contract at one time.

Soon, however, Fox became dissatisfied with merely purchasing the film product of other companies, and decided to embark on film production of his own. Fox first sent J. Gordon Edwards (grandfather of Blake Edwards), already a stage director, to study methods of film production in Europe, where Edwards placed under contract the Danish star Betty Nansen. On his return to New York, Edwards was appointed supervising director on all future Fox productions.

Edwards's first film was *Life's Shop Window,* filmed under the immediate direction of Henry Behlmer, and starring Claire Whitney and Stuart Holmes. *Life's Shop Window* proved to be a considerable success, so much so that Fox decided to add a further director to his payroll—his choice was Frank Powell from American Biograph. Powell in 1915 immediately commenced work on his first production for Fox, *A Fool There Was*. His star was **THEDA BARA**.

There is a great deal of truth in Dewitt Bodeen's remark that "without Theda Bara the Fox Film Corporation could not have gained the eminence in the motion picture industry it did."[2] Miss Bara was in fact born Theodosia Goodman in Cincinnati, Ohio on July 29, 1890, the daughter of a Jewish tailor. The name Theda Bara, an anagram of Arab Death, was chosen for her by two press-agents, Johnny Goldfrap and Al Selig. She was a sensation, and shocked the American public by her behaviour; smoking in public, burning incense in her room, etc. Even the newspapermen believed the fantastic stories that were put out about her power over men, and some reporters refused to be left alone in the same room as her for fear that she

Theda Bara in A FOOL THERE WAS

might seduce them. Her first film, *A Fool There Was,* was the story of a promising diplomat who is lured away from his home, wife and child by "the leading lady of the Theatre Antoine in Paris." The diplomat dies in Miss Bara's arms at the end after her request to "kiss me you fool." In the closing scene, Miss Bara is seen scattering rose petals on the unfortunate diplomat's lifeless body. The story was based on a play by Porter Emerson Browne, which in turn was adapted from Kipling's poem *The Vampire.*

A Fool There Was is the only one of Miss Bara's thirty-nine Fox films that is known to exist today. Twenty-two of those missing films were directed by J. Gordon Edwards. Something of the contents of those films can be gathered from their titles—*The Darling of Paris, The Tiger Woman, Cleopatra, When A Woman Sins,* and *When Men Desire.* Of Edwards, Miss Bara has said, he "was kind and considerate

J. Gordon Edwards

Theda Bara in CLEOPATRA (1917)

and the nicest director I ever had."[2] It was Edwards who later directed Betty Blythe in *The Queen of Sheba,* also for Fox, and made Miss Blythe the sex symbol of her time.

In 1921 Theda Bara married Charles Brabin, who had directed her in two films of 1919, *Kathleen Mavourneen* and *La Belle Russe.* Brabin had entered the film industry as a director with Edison in 1908. He proved himself a competent director in later years with *Stella Maris* (1926), *Call of the Flesh* (1930) and *The Mask of Fu Manchu* (1932). In the last, Brabin showed that he was more than capable of directing a work seething with eroticism, something that he had failed to achieve with any of his wife's vehicles. Brabin retired in 1938, and died in 1957.

Left: Charles Brabin

Right: Herbert Brenon

Miss Bara, it should be pointed out, did not entirely devote her talents to vamp roles. She was quite capable of portraying demure heroines. Hence her starring role in *The Two Orphans,* playing the role later portrayed by Lillian Gish in *Orphans of the Storm.* Miss Bara's film career ended with a Hal Roach comedy, in which she sent up the type of film that she had helped so very much to make popular. She died on April 7, 1955. Shortly before her death, Miss Bara tried to explain the popularity of her films: "To understand those days you must consider that people believed what they saw on the screen. Nobody had destroyed the grand illusion."[2]

The director of *The Two Orphans* was **HERBERT BRENON**, who, like Theda Bara, was to have a very important influence on the success of the Fox Company. Brenon was born in Dun Laoghaire, Ireland on January 13, 1880, and emigrated to America at the age of sixteen. His first job in his adopted country was as an office boy for Joseph Vivian, the theatrical agent. Following upon this, Brenon became a call boy at Dalys Theatre. Eventually, in 1909, he became a scenario writer cum editor with the Imp Company. It was three years before he directed his first film, *All for Her,* a one-reel story of the love and sacrifice of two old musicians for a small girl, featuring George Ober.

Brenon both acted in and directed many Imp productions, including the Company's first three-reeler *Leah the Forsaken,* with Leah Baird.

In May 1913, Brenon and his leading man, King Baggott, came to England, and here they filmed two productions, *Across the Atlantic* and *Ivanhoe.* The former featured a famous aviator of the day, Claude Graham White. *Ivanhoe* was a very spectacular production, filmed at Chepstow Castle, Monmouth, and based, rather loosely, on the novel by Sir Walter Scott. King Baggott portrayed the title role, Leah Baird was Rebecca of York and Herbert Brenon himself played Isaac of York. *Illustrated Films Monthly* prophesied, "*Ivanhoe,* in pictures will prove epoch-making in the history of cinematography in these islands and over the whole world." Brenon continued on his film-making tour of Europe, and in Paris filmed *Absinthe,* again with King Baggott, and then moved on to Germany to shoot three films starring William E. Shay.

Brenon's most famous film for the Imp Company was of course *Neptune's Daughter,* which was to make a star of Annette Kellerman. Seven reels in length, *Neptune's Daughter* was shot over a period of three months in Bermuda at a cost of $50,000. Others involved in this fantasy of the sea were William Welsh (as Neptune), William E. Shay (as King William) and Leah Baird (as Countess Olga).

In December 1914 Brenon parted company with Imp and formed his own producing company, Tiffany. The following year, he joined the William Fox organisation, for whom he first directed two Theda Bara vehicles, the aforementioned *The Two Orphans* and *The Kreutzer Sonata.* It was not until August 1915 that Brenon embarked on his most ambitious production yet.

Taking with him Annette Kellerman, Stuart Holmes and William Shay, Brenon sailed for Jamaica to direct *A Daughter of the Gods.* Nine months were taken over the shooting of the picture. Tales of Brenon's extravagance began to reach the ears of William Fox, and he was stunned by what he heard. A complete concrete and steel city was built on the site of the disused Island fortress of St. Augusta; a "White City" was erected at a cost of £50,000, afterwards to be destroyed by fire; 20,000 people were said to be engaged on the picture at one time and over 223,000 feet of Film were shot.

The cost of the entire production was claimed to be in the neigh-

Annette Kellerman in A DAUGHTER OF THE GODS

bourhood of £200,000. Fox was furious. He ordered Brenon's name to be removed from the credits of the film, and had the picture re-edited by Hettie Grey Baker (later to become editor-in-chief on all Fox productions). Brenon left the Fox organisation after unsuccessfully contesting in court that Fox had no right to tamper with his picture.

Despite Fox's orginal misgivings, *A Daughter of the Gods* was a tremendous success. Miss Kellerman created a sensation by appearing in the nude—some five years previous she had created a similar sensation by appearing in a one-piece bathing costume. Eighty-one year old Annette Kellerman is still active today producing underwater films for American television, and claims that she still swims half-a-mile a day.

Herbert Brenon went on to work for other companies, and directed, amongst others, *War Brides* with Nazimova, *The Passing of the Third Floor Back* with Sir Johnston Forbes-Robertson, *The Spanish Dancer* with Pola Negri, and the two delightful J. M. Barrie fantasies with Betty Bronson, *Peter Pan* and *A Kiss for Cinderella*. He returned to Britain in the mid-Thirties to direct a number of insignificant productions. As George Geltzer has pointed out, Brenon was known for his delicate and sentimental style of directing, "the Brenon style." He died in Los Angeles on June 21, 1958.

The later career of William Fox does not come within the scope of this book. Suffice it to say, that his studios in the Twenties were responsible for such films as John Ford's *The Iron Horse,* Murnau's *Sunrise,* and the teaming of Charles Farrell and Janet Gaynor in *Seventh Heaven* and other Frank Borzage films. Fox lost control of his company in the early Thirties as a result of his desire—one might almost say his greed—to control the entire motion picture industry. He died, still a very wealthy man, on May 8, 1952. *The Motion Picture Herald* described him as "one of the fighting greats of the film industry."

With William Fox, **CARL LAEMMLE** was the most important of the independent film-makers. Laemmle's Universal studios remained intact longer than the studio empires of any of his contemporaries. Today, Universal is the oldest of the major Hollywood studios.

German-born Carl Laemmle, like all his fellow film producers, built up his empire the hard way. He had emigrated to the U.S.A., and

Carl Laemmle

started work as a book-keeper in a clothing store in Oshkosh, Wisconsin. Through hard work, he became manager of the concern and managed to save $2,500. In 1905 he threw up his job in the clothing trade and decided to go into business for himself. The following year on February 24, he opened his first cinema in Chicago.

Six months later, Laemmle had opened several more cinemas and had become a film renter. In 1908, he imported from Germany the Synchroscope, "the only device which makes the moving picture machine and the phonograph work in perfect unison." It was sold outright to theatres for $395.

William Swanson, a fellow renter, announced on March 20, 1909 that he did not recognise the power of the Patents Company, and that he was now an independent film renter. On April 12 of the same year Carl Laemmle followed suit, and when the supply of films from the Patents Company dried up he announced the formation of the Independent Motion Picture Company (Imp). Laemmle baited the Patents Company by placing advertisements in the trade papers such as "Good Morrow—Have you paid $2 license to pick your teeth?"

The first Imp production was released on October 25, 1909. It was *Hiawatha,* based on Longfellow's poem, 988 ft. in length, and featured Gladys Hulette and William V. Ranous. The latter, formerly with the Vitagraph Company, also directed. In the advertisement for his new film, Laemmle said, "Film exchanges and exhibitors by the hundreds have been urging me to hurry up with this first release, but to all alike I have said: 'None of the going-off-half-cocked business for mine!' I have held back week after week to be absolutely certain that everything is in ship shape. Get *Hiawatha* and see if you don't agree that it starts a brand new era in American moving pictures. My motto will be: the best films that man's ingenuity can devise and the best films man's skill can execute."

At this time, the most popular player with the American Biograph Company—indeed the most popular player in films—was **FLORENCE LAWRENCE**. As companies belonging to the Patents Company group did not encourage unwarranted personal publicity for their players, Miss Lawrence's name was not known to the general public. Filmgoers knew her only as "The Biograph Girl."

In 1910, Carl Laemmle engineered perhaps the first publicity stunt the cinema was to know when he stole Miss Lawrence away from Bio-

Florence Lawrence

graph and put her under contract to Imp. He then ran a story in the St. Louis newspapers that Florence Lawrence had died in a street car accident. Following upon this, Laemmle announced in advertisements in *Moving Picture World* of March 12, 1910: "The blackest and at the same time the silliest lie yet circulated by the enemies of IMP was the story foisted on the public of St. Louis last week to the effect Miss Lawrence, "The Imp Girl," formerly known as "The Biograph Girl" had been killed by a street car. It was a black lie so cowardly. We now announce our next film *The Broken Path*." Miss Lawrence also made a personal appearance in St. Louis and was mobbed by her fans. Laemmle also acquired from American Biograph Miss Lawrence's husband and director, Harry Salter, and her leading man King Baggott.

Florence Lawrence was to become one of the forgotten stars of the cinema. In the Thirties she was one of the "old-timers" on pension at M-G-M. She received a small weekly salary and occasionally appeared in crowd scenes. She committed suicide in January 1939.

Another Biograph player to be lured away to Imp was Mary Pickford, who came with her leading man and future husband Owen Moore. Her first film for Imp was *Their First Misunderstanding,* directed by Imp's new director Thomas Ince. The capture of Mary Pickford was followed by a publicity campaign, in which Laemmle announced "Little Mary is an Imp Now!" It was war between Imp and the Patents Company, and for a while Imp was forced to leave America and produce its pictures in Cuba.

Imp productions were favourably received by the critics. One wrote: "There are at most six persons in these little playlets, and always the same ones are used; they are young, good-looking and not only good actors, but excellent pantomimists (and surely that is a fact worth recording). The faces of these young people are wholly new to me, and in a period of a few weeks, I have witnessed as many as eight widely different, and thoroughly well conceived plays with fully as much plot, and better by far interpretation than is given to the speaking playlets in our best vaudeville theatres."

June 8, 1912 saw the formation of the Universal Film Manufacturing Company, with Carl Laemmle as president. Universal was formed by the amalgamation of the Imp Company; Pat Power's Power's Picture Plays (founded in 1909) and Adam Kessel and Charles Bauman's Bison Life Motion Pictures (also founded in 1909). The first release of the new company was *The Dawn of Netta,* directed by Tom Ricketts. Also in 1912, Juliet Shelby made her first screen appearance in a one-reeler *The Nurse.* Miss Shelby was later to become Mary Miles Minter. The same year, Laemmle took his filming operations to California.

Terry Ramsaye claims that Universal were responsible for discovering the box-office potential of sex when in 1913 they released *Traffic in Souls,* directed by George Loane Tucker and starring Jane Gail and Matt Moore. The story was concerned with white slavery, and was based on the Rockefeller White Slavery Report and the investigation of the Vice Trust by District Attorney Whitman. It cost $5,700 to produce; it grossed $450,000.[25]

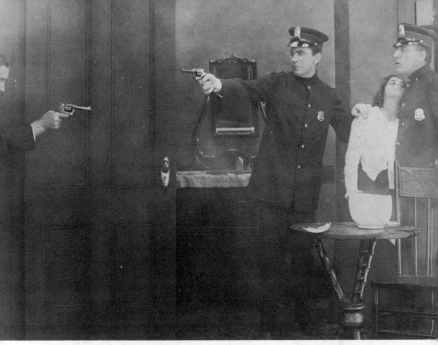

Matt Moore (policeman holding gun) in TRAFFIC IN SOULS

The film's director, George Loane Tucker, came to England later in 1913 as a director for the London Film Company. He died in 1921. The writer and producer of *Traffic in Souls* was an Irishman, Walter McNamara, who seemed to have specialised in controversial films. The following year he directed *Ireland a Nation,* which was banned by the English authorities in Ireland, and which some claim may have been partly responsible for sparking off the 1916 Easter Rebellion in Dublin.

Universal sent a camera crew to Nassau in the Bahamas in 1914 to film the Williamson Submarine Corporation's vessel *Jules Verne* in action, and also to record life on the sea bed. *The Cinema* commented, "To photograph the bottom of the sea is, perhaps, the last of the big things to be done on this hoary planet." Some of the scenes shot on this expedition were put to use the following year in *The Submarine Spy*.

The most important event in Carl Laemmle's life occurred on March 15, 1915 when he opened Universal City. The studios were situated at the 230 acre Taylor Ranch on the Los Angeles River, some five miles north of Hollywood, in what was then Lankershim. The opening was a day for history. Twenty thousand onlookers gathered on Lankershim Boulevard to watch Universal's lady police chief Laura Oakley present Carl Laemmle with the golden key to the City. A brass band played "The Star Spangled Banner," and the Stars and Stripes were unfurled on a flagpole in the centre of the City. Thomas A. Edison and Henry Ford motored down to dedicate the first artificially lighted stage, and the entire event was filmed by U. K. Whipple. At the same time, another new Universal studio was opened at Fort Lee, New Jersey. Two hundred and fifty films were produced at Universal City in the first twelve months of its existence; the first film to be made here being *Damon and Pythias* with Herbert Rawlinson and Cleo Madison.

In 1916, Anna Pavlova journeyed to Universal City to film *The Dumb*

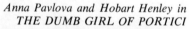

Anna Pavlova and Hobart Henley in
THE DUMB GIRL OF PORTICI

Girl of Portici, under the direction of Lois Weber, with Douglas Gerrard, Boris Karloff (making his screen *début*) and the Russian Ballet. The film was an adaptation of Auber's *Masaniello.* One critic wrote of Pavlova's performance: "Pavlova's individual part is magnificent, having all the sincerity and charm of realisation in her work, and the great gift of being able to present her portrayal by—as we have already said—the poetry of motion."

In the same year, Miss Weber was also responsible for *Where Are My Children?,* starring Tyrone Power Snr. The film showed "the wrecking of happiness and health when, as is unfortunately only too true, evil practices are resorted to in marriage." The "evil practices" in question were abortion and contraception. The couple in the film, an attorney and his wife, were childless because of "a quack doctor's activities," and the film ends with a scene of the couple in old age, alone and "without children to comfort." One reviewer likened it to Maeterlinck's *The Blue Bird.*

Turning from the subject of sexual practices, Universal in 1916 released *A Silent Conquest,* directed by Jack Conway, with J. Warren Kerrigan and Lois Wilson. A moral piece on the evils of alcohol, *A Silent Conquest* showed "the power of love to quench the desire for drink."

Aside from Conway and Miss Weber, Universal's directors at this time included Frank Lloyd, Robert Z. Leonard, Frank Borzage, Elmer Clifton, Allan Holubar, Edward LeSaint, Joseph De Grasse, Francis Ford, W. S. Van Dyke and Rupert Julian. The last directed one of the first anti-German war films to come out of America, *The Kaiser— The Beast of Berlin,* with Julian as the Kaiser.

All Universal productions throughout the period covered by this book were released in Great Britain under the trademark of "Trans-Atlantic."

Carl Laemmle remained president of Universal until 1936, when he sold out his interest in the firm and retired. He died in September 1939 at the age of seventy-two. Will H. Hays said of him: "The services of Carl Laemmle to the motion picture industry were distinguished. He had courage and vision and he kept his honour bright. He fought for what he believed to be right and kept his plighted word. He gave more than he asked. His friendship braved the storm. Carl Laemmle had and deserved the deep personal affection of all who knew him."

6. American Biograph and Griffith

DURING THE PERIOD 1908–1913, it was **DAVID WARK GRIFFITH** who began to discover for himself and use all the techniques that were to make the culmination of it such a revolutionary one when he shot *The Birth of a Nation* and *Intolerance*. In the scores of films he made for Biograph can be found ideas in embryo which would blossom to their full maturity in his two great masterpieces and be used again and be perfected further still in the pictures he made after 1917 and continued to make until 1931.

When looking at these films for the first time, one is immediately struck by the diversity of subject matter (over five hundred films in four years is no mean achievement in itself), but also by their similarity. A lot of this is due to Griffith's already highly-developed visual sense, which is clear and obvious in all the films. But another factor is the manner in which the same themes crop up and are used in variant forms.

Much criticism has been levelled at Griffith for relying too heavily on what has become known as "the Griffith Last-Minute Rescue," and it is true that the chase and rescue in the closing minutes of a film figure a great deal in his work, but to maintain that he *relied* on this is clearly criticism without basis. The injustice of such an accusation becomes clear when one examines the films themselves. Quite often, the last-minute rescue simply *doesn't rescue*. In *The Massacre* (1912), for example, the cavalry, racing to relieve a wagon train from an attack by Indians thirsty for revenge, arrives in time only to count the corpses of the entire train except a mother and her child. Indeed, the complete failure of the last-minute rescue is not unknown in his work. In *Intolerance,* both the French and Babylonian "rescues" fail.

Griffith often turned to literature for the subjects of his early films. Naturally, these rarely culminated in a chase. So Griffith showed many times that he was in no way dependent on a chase for the interest in his pictures which he required of his audiences. Often he made the bold step of treating serious social subjects, and the films in this category clearly do not require a chase or rescue with which to conclude.

D. W. Griffith

Arthur Johnson and Florence Lawrence in
A RACE FOR A LIFE (frame enlargement)

There are many, many pictures which do not contain either a chase or a rescue. One, *The Little Teacher* (1911) illustrates how Griffith was supremely capable of tackling an extremely simple story and avoiding any big dramatic climaxes, whilst producing a film of extraordinary quality.

Mary Pickford plays a young school teacher who suffers at the hand of the school bully, Dave. She is on the point of tears when she meets by chance a surveyor, in whom she confides her troubles. When the surveyor introduces Mary to his wife, she is heart-broken. But Dave comforts her with a small bouquet of flowers, and, as elsewhere in his films, Griffith uses flowers to symbolise purity and sincerity. The subtitle, "Two bouquets—the simple country blossoms are the best."

Griffith shows in this totally unpretentious film his ability to create a strong atmosphere without a strong narrative line. Later on, in *True Heart Susie*, he demonstrated the same ability on a larger scale. No

*Mary Pickford in SO NEAR YET
SO FAR (frame enlargement)*

need here for the thrilling chase or rescue to end on; the simple country blossoms are the best!

Even those films which *do* contain a chase or a rescue hardly resemble one another because of it. In fact it doesn't always follow that a film which involves a rescue automatically contains a chase, or vice versa. *So Near Yet So Far* (1912) is a film in which all the main action is contained within two rooms on either side of the hall. And yet Mary Pickford is rescued from the clutches of burglars by Walter Miller just the same, and the result is none the less exciting for being confined.

In *A Drive for a Life* (1909), the rescue relies on what could be described as more obvious techniques, as the title suggests. The rescue is constructed in such a way that one cannot fail to be caught up in the urgent excitement it creates, nor to be impressed by the panache with which it is handled. The whole rescue takes place only in the last thirteen shots, which begin with Arthur Johnson's discovering that his jealous ex-mistress has poisoned a box of chocolates and sent them to his *fiancée*. He rushes out to his car and jumps in, yelling instructions to his chauffeur as they pull away from the house. Simultaneously, we see a messenger arriving at Florence Lawrence's house to deliver the deadly chocolates. A shot of the car speeding along the road is then followed by Florence's receiving the chocolates and beginning to open the box. Then . . . the car jogs stubbornly to a halt, and Johnson jumps out with his chauffeur and they dash round to the bonnet. As the chauffeur fiddles with the engine in an attempt to repair the breakdown, Johnson is almost beside himself. At last the chauffer announces all is well. They both climb back in, and the car speeds off once again. Meanwhile, Florence is lifting the lid from the box, selecting a chocolate, and raising it to her mouth . . . at which point we are jolted back to a scene which seems to have little or no relevance to the urgent and dramatic situation. A peaceful road scene, with a barrier gate being opened by a gatekeeper for a horse-drawn carriage to pass through. The keeper closes the gate, waves to the carriage and walks out of the picture. As he does so, we see Johnson's car come racing round the bend in the distance and towards the barrier. It doesn't stop, but crashes straight through the gate, and out of the picture as the keeper runs up to his shattered barrier, shaking his fist at Johnson. Florence, by this time, has decided that the gift should be *fed* to her. So she hands the chocolate she was about to put in her mouth to her sister, who is then asked to feed it to Florence. The same horse-drawn carriage we saw passing through the gate in the previous scene is now trying to maneuvre into a side turning. But Johnson's car passes at great speed, just catching the edge of the carriage. The carriage wheels over and splinters across the road, while the car speeds on. Florence's sister accidentally drops the chocolate—the car is now racing frantically to arrive in time—and Johnson arrives at last, breathless, but in time to stop Florence from eating the fatal candy.

It is interesting to note here how, eight years before *Intolerance,* Griffith was already using those techniques which made that film the legendary work it has become. The intercutting of the two component actions in the closing sequence of *A Drive for a Life* is still of a primitive manner and bears no direct comparison with the infinitely more sophisticated editing in *Intolerance*. It is a straightforward interpolation of the car and its objective. But at the same time, Griffith is able to introduce elements which work *with* the treatment, or technique, without having to rely too heavily on the technique alone to provide all the excitement.

It is significant, therefore, that Griffith relied neither wholly on the content, or narrative line, nor wholly on the technique, or method of presentation, for dramatic effectiveness, but blended them together. In other words, he achieved a perfect cinematic whole. And this as early as 1909.

In *The Lesser Evil* (1912), Blanche Sweet is rescued from a launch after a chase across water. In *A Beast at Bay* (1911) Mary Pickford is rescued by her lover from the clutches of an escaped criminal. In *The Coming of Angelo* (1913) it is this time Blanche Sweet who rescues Walter Miller just before an explosion, meant for Miller, kills her rejected and jealous lover.

If these films were notable only because they contained the ageless excitement of a chase, it would be useless quoting them here. *The Lesser Evil; A Beast at Bay* and *The Coming of Angelo* all contain elements which make them exceptional works when put alongside other films of the period.

The Lesser Evil opens with Blanche Sweet on the beach with a girl friend (Mae Marsh in a small part) just about to leave for a rendezvous with her boy friend. We then see the boy friend himself, at work mending nets. (A film called *The Mender of Nets,* which will be discussed later, was completed by Griffith three months after *The Lesser Evil.*) Blanche leaves and makes her way towards an old log cabin on the foreshore, which we discover is a hideout for a gang of smugglers just arrived with their latest haul.

Blanche arrives, and is surprised to find her lover not there. She decides to look in the cabin to see if he is waiting for her inside, and walks straight into the gang of smugglers. The smugglers are left with no alternative but to take Blanche with them when they leave. The lover, meanwhile, has discovered that his watch has stopped and rushes in panic to the rendezvous, only in time to see the smugglers, with Blanche, disappearing out to sea.

He runs headlong to the nearest customs station, and together with several officers they set off in launches to catch the smugglers. On board the smugglers' boat, Blanche is locked in the captain's cabin. He comes in, and makes several efforts to kiss Blanche, but each time she manages to fend off his advances. Eventually he abandons the attempt,

Blanche Sweet and Wilfred Lucas in
THE LESSER EVIL (frame enlargement)

and turns to go, only to be faced by a mutinous crew. He locks himself in with Blanche and draws his pistol.

Meanwhile we see the launches racing in pursuit; spectacular tracking shots taken from another fast launch, the captain, firing on his mutinous crew, uses up all of his ammunition except for one bullet. He looks towards the terrified Blanche and shows her the gun. The Lesser Evil—death by his gun or dishonour when the crew manage to break into the cabin? This idea recurs in *The Battle at Elderbush Gulch* and again in *The Birth of a Nation*.

But the launches and officers arrive and the crew are arrested. For a moment it now seems that the captain himself has to choose between the lesser evil—but he manages to escape by diving off the boat and swimming ashore. Blanche and her lover are reunited, but there is a tantalisingly enigmatic shot showing Blanche peering through binoculars at the escaped captain, suggesting that she does not share the others' opinion that he is a rogue at all. The film ends with him staggering up the beach—the boat in the distance.

The chase in *A Beast at Bay* is particularly interesting for the marked resemblance it bears to the chase in the Modern Story of *Intolerance*. A chase between a car and a locomotive develops, in which shots from a moving vehicle in front of both the train and the car cannot fail to bring to mind the breathtaking sequence in *Intolerance*. One particular shot shows the car, with Mary Pickford and a convict in it, on one side of the picture, the locomotive on the other, belching smoke. In the middle of the frame, between the car and the train, there is a fairly wide brook, which reflects the train and smoke. It is an extraordinarily dynamic shot, and one that conveys the excitement of the chase precisely and with the visual economy that was to become so typical of Griffith in later years.

The Coming of Angelo presents a more unusual variation on the theme of chase or rescue. Blanche has forsaken Guido for Angelo, and such is Guido's grief that he sets a time-bomb off in his house in order to kill himself. A close-up of the clock face shows that it will explode in thirty minutes. But at that moment he sees Angelo walk past the window, and the title, "Why should I die for his happiness?" is followed by Guido's inviting Angelo back into the house. Blanche sees this from a distance, and is suspicious of her ex-lover's intentions. Another close-up of the watch face tells us that there are now only five minutes before the explosion. Blanche walks up to the house, and immediately another close-up shows three minutes to go. An extreme longshot shows Blanche on the hillside, standing a little way from the hut. Guido leaves the hut as Blanche arrives at the door, and a struggle ensues. A shot of the fuse is followed by an explosion. As the smoke clears we discover that Angelo had come out when he saw Guido and Blanche struggling, and Guido has been killed by the blast.

Certainly it is unusual to find the heroine in the role of rescuer and not rescued. But there are other elements of the cinematic treatment in this film which are unusual. In the passage quoted above, for example, Griffith uses a very sophisticated device to upset the spectator's equilibrium, and so add to the tenseness of the situation. From a very large close-up of the clock face, showing three minutes to go before the explosion, he cuts directly to an extreme long shot. The fact that one second we are shown a piece of information *forcefully* which causes us concern for the safety of Angelo and the next we are pulled right back to be given a long and objective view of the hill and the little hut with Blanche nearby, makes this technique in effect a kind of stalling, a refusal to provide the audience with a rapid conclusion.

This device is also used elsewhere in the film, and creates the same feeling of simultaneous detachment and involvement. When Blanche first falls for Angelo, they are together on a deserted beach. Unknown to them, Guido, who knows nothing of their infatuation, is not far away, behind a sea wall. An extreme long shot shows the pair on the beach. This is followed by a medium shot (that is, a shot which shows all of the figure or most of it) which is in turn followed by another extreme long shot in which the two embrace. A large close-up of Guido shows his reaction. Another medium shot of Blanche and Angelo is followed again with a close-up of Guido. Guido walks out of the shot and Griffith cuts again to the medium shot of the lovers, into which Guido walks to interrupt them.

At such a stage in the development of cinematic art, one does not altogether expect to encounter such advanced ideas; by July 1913 when this film was completed, Griffith had mastered the most sophisticated techniques of prompting reactions from his audience by the placing of the camera in relation to the characters. Not simply a close-up to register a reaction, but a far more advanced and precise method.

The Coming of Angelo contains themes and ideas, apart from the rescue, which occur—again in variant forms—in a number of quite different films. One of these is revenge, the other is jealousy. These two ideas, because they are instigators of a chase or rescue, occur just as frequently in Griffith's work. They are also indisputably legitimate sources of dramatic situations. In *The Squaw's Love Story* (*The Twilight Song*) (1911), which will be discussed in more detail later, revenge is the result of misunderstanding. In another Western, the revenge is of a more familiar kind. The Indian chief in *The Massacre* (1912) swears revenge on the White Man for the destruction of his village by cavalry. In *The Drive for a Life* revenge is itself the result of jealousy. *Fate's Interception* (1912) runs along similar lines, but is a little more subtle. Mary Pickford finds herself jilted, not for another woman, but for her *lover's job*. When West finds that he has been called home from Mexico after a long posting, he refuses to take his Mexican sweetheart with him. Mary turns to a gullible admirer to carry out her revenge.

110

Mary Pickford in FATE'S
INTERCEPTION (frame enlargement)

"Cut me the false love from the Americano's heart and I'll marry you,"
she says. The film ends with West and Mary reunited but, curiously
and rather unjustly, with the poor gullible admirer gassed in the room
where he was to have murdered West because of his love for Mary.

In *Fate* (1913), revenge is the result of humiliation. Sim, humiliated
in the eyes of his hooligan colleagues by being beaten by an old man,
plans to blow up the old man's hut, with his two grand-daughters in it.
Unknown to Sim, one of his colleagues—played by Bobby Harron—
stumbles drunkenly into the hut, drives out the two girls and begins
to help himself to the food, unaware of the fused barrel of gunpowder
in the next room. After a masterly sequence in which the tension is
built up slowly and meticulously, the hut explodes, Harron (in a part
uncharacteristic of him) and all. The old man is beside himself with
grief until he discovers the two girls safe, and Sim bitterly regrets his
action and realises his stupidity when he sees the corpse of Harron
among the wreckage. *The Mender of Nets* (1912) presents revenge in
which the two girls involved play absolutely passive roles. Tom leaves

111

Bobby Harron in FATE (frame enlargement)

Grace in order to become engaged to Mary, the net-mender. Grace's brother swears revenge for his sister's dishonour and a fight ensues between him and Tom. The questionable resolution of this film is that Mary, content that Tom should be happy even though it is not with herself, yields him back to Grace. There is a touching scene at the end of the picture in which Mary Pickford comforts Mabel Normand (Grace) before leaving her to Tom. Her last words are "I'll mend the nets."

In her autobiography, *When the Movies Were Young,* the first Mrs. D. W. Griffith (who was Linda Arvidson, a prominent Biograph actress) tells how Griffith was "always overly fastidious about 'location.' His feeling for charming landscapes and his use of them in the movies was a significant factor in the success of his early pictures."

No less a significant factor in his subsequent feature-length films either, it should be added. A lot of the pictorial beauty in the Biographs is attributable in equal measure to Griffith's gifted cameraman, G. W. Bitzer. His skill in motion picture photography was as advanced at that time as were Griffith's own ideas of motion picture direction. But it should be assumed that Griffith chose exactly *what* should be photographed, and it is this factor that counts most. There are numerous examples of striking "set pieces" in Griffith's early films, which are easily comparable to modern films considered to be visually beautiful.

The Coming of Angelo opens with a stunning series of shots giving a photographic "study" of the environment in which the story takes place. We see Blanche Sweet walking across headlands with the sea washing the shore below the cliffs, and the wide panoramas from the hilltops of the small fishing village and the surrounding countryside and coast. The picture begins with a shot in which only a part of the frame is used, and then "irises" out to include the rest of the panorama, filling the entire screen area. This is a technique used extensively by Griffith, and to extremely effective ends.

This is one example of the way in which Griffith understood and exploited the medium of film. His visual sense; as translated by Bitzer for the screen, is one of the first points we note in these pre-1913 Biograph films—"ABs"—and is the main element in all of them which is never absent. The technical expertise, the relatively sophisticated performances he coaxed from his players, these are also important factors in the explanation of his importance as an artist; but alongside these, he knew and appreciated visual beauty. In 1947, he passed judgement on sound films (of which he had made but two): "What the modern movie lacks is beauty—the beauty of moving wind in trees, the little movement in the beautiful blowing on the blossoms in the trees." Even his quasi-poetical turn of phrase suggests the passion for beauty which he was unable to find in the work of his successors.

When he talked of "moving wind in trees," perhaps he was thinking of his 1912 AB, *The Beast at Bay,* the very first shot of which is one of a mass of leaves, blowing gently in a summer breeze. He uses this opening shot, as it happens, as a foil for the real subject of the film, which is an escaped convict on the run. After the shot has been allowed to run for some considerable length of time, and we have fully recognised the intrinsic pleasure of the image, a hand appears, pulls the leaves aside and the convict, dirty and recognisably evil, emerges slowly from the bushes.

In the opening sequences of *Fate's Interception* (1912), when West meets Mary and the pair walk together through glades of willows, the photography achieves an extraordinary pitch of beauty. The scene is free of sub-titles, and one shot, taken from above, shows West embracing Mary beneath the willows, which are so composed in the frame as to isolate the two lovers while surrounding them with the soft, natural curves of the branches. This adds a kind of sensuality to the scene.

Griffith's love for pictorial beauty can be seen in the magnificent splendour of Belshazzar's Babylon in *Intolerance* as the culmination of these small and unpretentious settings and locations in which he chose to place his early dramas. We have already described in some detail the relatively elaborate devices of film editing he employed in, for example, *The Coming of Angelo,* when he began cutting from extreme long shot to close-up. But in *The Drive for a Life* can be seen the fact that Griffith also understood right from the beginning of his career in film-making, that not only one *cutting* of the shots together, but the continuous action within one shot held for a considerable length of time also determined the emotional response of an audience. *The Drive for a Life* contains a long and ambitious (bearing in mind the film was made in 1909) "tracking," or moving, shot, which begins with the camera stationery facing the open car in which Arthur Johnson and Florence Lawrence are travelling towards us. As it gets closer to us, the camera begins to track backwards, just in front of the car. After a while, a horse-drawn carriage, with Johnson's former mistress in it, swings into view just behind the car, without either Johnson or Florence noticing it. The carriage follows them for a while, the camera still travelling before the vehicles, keeping both of them all the time in view. Eventually the car picks up speed and draws out of the shot on the right as it overtakes the camera, leaving only the horse and carriage in shot. Both the camera and carriage stop simultaneously, the carriage then manoeuvers a "U" turn and drives off into the distance away from the camera. The shot ends with an interrupted pan to the right, suggesting that the shot was formerly even longer and more complex than is described here. It would be an injustice to assume that Griffith did not merely rely on editing to put over a dramatic point— quite the contrary, as the shot above illustrates, he recognised the effectiveness of containing an important action within one, uninterrupted "take" as much as that of quick, staccato cutting.

"They have forgotten entirely," said Griffith (quoted in Ezra Goodman's *The Fifty Year Decline and Fall of Hollywood*), "They have forgotten that no still painting—not the greatest ever—was anything but a still picture. But the moving picture! Today they have forgotten movement in the moving picture—it is all still and stale." This statement by Griffith is admirably backed up by his films—from as early as 1909—and when he said all this in 1947, one year before his death, he still regarded himself as the man who taught Hollywood the principles of its trade—principles that included the ability to create something beautiful. Hollywood chose to ignore him and his genius only because it changed and he refused to change with it. He ceased to be able to produce films that would make money, because he did not subscribe to the policy of pandering to his public. But Griffith's criticisms of Hollywood were not entirely prompted by bitterness. He had a lot to complain about. He also had beauty on his side. "We have," he said, still including himself in the active film industry despite the fact that he had not made a film himself for over fifteen years, "taken beauty and exchanged it for stilted voices."

Erich von Stroheim, who always considered himself a pupil of Griffith's and acknowledged his debt to Griffith until the end of his life, described him in a radio broadcast as "The first man who had put beauty and poetry into a cheap and tawdry sort of amusement which some people had shamefacedly accepted while waiting for a train or to seek shelter from the inclemencies of the weather."

But if his audiences had accepted Griffith's films "shamefacedly" in 1908, by August 1913, when he left Biograph for an independent career, they had become works which many movie directors had taken as models and aspired to equal.

Griffith never looked further than the commonplace for the situations in his best films. Young love was a favourite subject, since the idyllic imagery it demanded for his public appealed immensely to him. Wherever there is a pair of lovers in an AB, we may be sure that there is also a misunderstanding, or a jealous rival, or perhaps an obligation on the part of one partner or the other that stands between them and the course of true love.

Misunderstandings appear not infrequently in the ABs. Sometimes they are precepts for attempted revenge on a suspected lover of the wife, as is the case in *The Voice of a Child* (1911). The misunderstanding in this film is more complicated than usual, and eventually results in the husband suspecting his wife of infidelity, who in turn suspects him of the same thing. It is Blanche who first becomes suspicious when she discovers him with his arm around his stenographer. She in any case feels neglected as a result of his involvement with his work and immediately draws her own conclusions from the scene. However, the stenographer, bribed by an old college friend of the husband's who himself has designs on Blanche, secretly plants a photograph of a girl in his pocket. An interesting point here is that Griffith shows us the child watching the stenographer place the photograph in his father's pocket—thus giving the child the only true "major" role in the film, inasmuch as he is the central character because he knows what all the others do not—a knowledge he shares with us, the audience. As a result of this, therefore, it is with him that we identify most, since it is with him that we naturally entrust the satisfactory outcome of the film.

A similar situation is to be found in *The Root of Evil* (1912), where

Mary Pickford and Wilfred Lucas in HOME FOLKS

Bobby Harron (at right) in A MISUNDERSTOOD BOY

the child is the key figure in the outcome of the film. An unscrupulous adviser attempts to poison the rich father of a girl and therefore make off with his fortune. The girl's child, however, innocently imitates the advisor and switches glasses, thus reversing the position of the poisoned drink and killing off the adviser.

In *Home Folks* (1911), a misunderstanding arises when Mary's husband sees her kissing her brother, whom she has not seen for some considerable time, and whom he has not seen at all. *The Squaw's Love* includes a misunderstanding when White Eagle's attempts to reunite

Wild Flower (Mabel Normand) and her lover are misinterpreted by his own girl, who becomes insanely jealous of Normand, for whom it would seem White Eagle has deserted her.

In *A Misunderstood Boy* (1913), the central idea of misunderstanding bears a remarkable resemblance to a scene in *Intolerance,* and it is fairly safe to presume that this film is one of the many that provide the roots to Griffith's greatest triumph in film-making. Bobby Harron plays the central character in both films. In *A Misunderstood Boy,* he is witness to the murder of a gold prospector by gangsters. When he goes to aid the dying man, however, the police arrive and he becomes the suspect for the murder.

There is a brilliant case of misunderstanding in *His Daughter* (1911). In his haste to show a photograph to a friend, William's father slips and injures himself. William's sweetheart decides to look after the old man, but her drunken father has other ideas. He disguises himself and sets about robbing the invalid of his life's savings. Mary tries to stop him, unaware that the intruder is her own father. This misunderstanding has a truly pathetic and tragic meaning.

There can be no reasonable doubt that Griffith saw the motion picture as a powerful weapon against social injustices. He used it as such many times, in the many ABs he made with a social subject as their theme, and his sense of social realism also became evident in his feature films of later years.

A widely quoted example of this type of film is *A Corner in Wheat,* (1909). Adapted from a story by the celebrated American novelist Frank Norris, (whose realism was later to provide Erich von Stroheim with the source for his masterpiece *Greed*) it is a film of simple but effective contrasts between affluence and poverty.

In April of the same year Griffith made *A Drunkard's Reformation* which is also celebrated by some extraordinarily beautiful photography, especially in some sombre fire-side scenes.

Gold Is Not All (1910), like *A Corner in Wheat,* also makes meaningful comparison between rich and poor, coming out very much in favour of the poor, and simple, life. While the rich girl's marriage is about to break up, the poor girl is blissfully happy with her husband. A title describes the peasant's home as "The cottage where love abides"—Griffith often used a title of this nature in his films to presage a scene of simple, austere, yet idyllic happiness, and we see the poor

THE SQUAW'S LOVE

Courtesy of David Robinson

husband bring his wife a modest bouquet of flowers (cf. *The Little Teacher*).

The young daughter of the rich girl falls dangerously ill, but although the girl offers all she owns, the doctors find that they are unable to cure the child's illness. A shot of the poor family dancing is followed by a scene in which the doctor slowly and solemnly pulls the sheet up over the dead child's face, while the young mother stands helplessly by. Griffith ends the film on a literary note. The title,

> "Riches cannot rescue from the grave
> Which claims alike Monarch and the slave."

points to Griffith's belief in racial and social equality, a belief that was to come into such violent question five years later when *The Birth of a Nation* was first seen.

All the vivid realism to be found in his great masterpieces can be traced back six years or more to its source in the few films he made early in his career with a social question as their theme. And we can trace the development and perfection of this approach from *A Drunkard's Reformation* through those titles already mentioned, plus many more in the years before 1913, to the famous *Musketeers of Pig Alley* which still retains such a degree of realism that it appears hardly to have dated at all. The striking realism of this film can certainly be seen as an indication of the style that Griffith was to employ with such success in *Intolerance*.

It is perhaps worth mentioning, while discussing this film, Griffith's approach to the representation of these subjects. In a letter written by him in 1917 he said, "How are we to depict the right unless we show the wrong? Unless we show the evils of a vicious past, how are we allowed to be the means of guiding the footsteps of the present generation?"

Many of the pictures made during this period concern themselves with the responsibility of one marriage partner to the other. In *The Voice of a Child,* already mentioned briefly, it is the wife who eventually sees the folly of her own actions and at the last minute decides not to run off with her husband's college friend but recognises her responsibility to her child and husband.

In *A Flash of Light* (1910), it is again the wife who appears as the inconstant partner. The story involves a chemist who is blinded in an explosion. A title, following scenes of his wife trying to help her now sightless and helpless husband, reads, ANNOYED BY HIS HELPLESSNESS SHE EASILY ACCEPTS DIVERSION, and is followed by a scene in which she is offered a part on the stage. A title compresses the action: SHE LEAVES HER HUSBAND FOR THE OUTSIDE WORLD'S GLITTER.

While his wife, Belle, is intending to divorce, he undergoes a successful operation for the restoration of his sight. In a highly dramatic scene, Belle cautiously approaches her husband as his bandages are removed. But when he moves towards her in recognition, she retreats to the drawn curtains in horror. The curtain at which she tugs falls to the ground, and rays of sunlight stream into the room and also into the chemist's still vulnerable eyes. For the second time, and now permanently, he is blinded. Belle's sister, who had taken her place in the interim when Belle was away, is near at hand and eventually the chemist finds her to be a true wife.

Griffith returned to a similar theme the next year in *Through*

The chemist is blinded in A FLASH OF LIGHT (frame enlargement)

Darkened Vales, in which Blanche Sweet loses her sight in an explosion of a chafing dish. Her husband also becomes blind as a result of overwork supporting her. All ends happily however, when he saves enough money to pay for an operation in which Blanche regains her sight.

A parallel theme is that of responsibility to one's parents. In *A Plainsong* (1910), Mary Pickford plays the only daughter of an elderly couple (Kate Bruce and Walter Miller). One day the lonely daughter meets a stranger who tries to persuade her to go away with him. She declines, however, preferring to stay with her ageing parents. The manager, undaunted, tries to win her with jealousy, and after the title, THE GREAT TEMPTATION, Mary decides to go away with him. She leaves a letter of explanation for her Mother—her Father is blind—and leaves to meet the stranger at the station. While waiting on the platform, she sees a group of old men and women walking by. The title REMEMBER THY MOTHER AND THY

Kate Bruce, Walter Christy Miller and Mary Pickford in A PLAINSONG (frame enlargement)

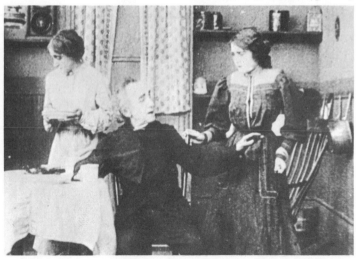

FATHER illustrates her state of mind, and this is further revealed to us when Griffith cuts back to her parents sitting alone in a room. Mary immediately picks up her bags and the stranger arrives with the tickets, although not in time to stop her catching the tram home. As she arrives, the blind father accidentally happens to find the note on the table. Thinking that Mary is his wife, he hands it to her. She tears it up, breathing a sigh of relief before dimming the lamp, which acts also as a fade-out and the end of the film. It is a simple but extraordinarily powerful film, powerful in the sense that its philosophy is one which appeals to the heart immediately and spontaneously: we all at one time or another have felt this deep sense of responsibility to our parents, and Griffith crystallises this sense perfectly and simply, as the title suggests.

The Unwelcome Guest (1913) is constructed along similar lines as *A Plainsong* where the situation is dependent on friction between generations. Mary Pickford alone is faithful to the old man, whilst his own children treat him without respect. Into this category falls also *Home Folks* (1911) in which a stern father runs his household on "what he thinks the Bible precepts," and consequently drives his son to run away in desperation.

Another case of irresponsibility in marriage is seen in *Oil and Water* (1913). After a visit to a theatre by a wealthy but "idealist" minded gentleman, (Henry B. Walthall), to see a dance on a Grecian theme, he is captivated by the lead dancer, played by Blanche Sweet. In the audience can be seen Lillian and Dorothy Gish, playing minor supporting roles. The dance itself in an exotic style not dissimilar to the dance sequences in the Babylonian story in *Intolerance,* includes a lot of very complex choreography.

After the performance, Walthall proposes to Blanche, and she accepts. Following the title, HIS WIFE, he is shown ushering Blanche into his home, thus giving the sense perfectly of a rushed, impetuous wedding. It also serves, of course, to compress the action: but consider the absence of a lengthy title explaining his marriage, and also the wider, and more ironic, use of this particularly curt title.

Before long Blanche begins to feel repressed in the level-headed and sober household, and feels the need for the excitement her former life held for her. This is brought to a head when she throws a tantrum while her husband wants to read and study. And when

123

Charles Mailes and Blanche Sweet in OIL AND WATER

three of her former theatrical friends come to visit her and the talk turns to the latest dance craze, Blanche and Walthall have a vicious argument after the friends have departed. She decides to leave him, even at the cost of having to surrender the custody of their only child to him.

The film draws to a close with a sequence full of comparisons and parallels vividly illustrating the title. A scene in a musical play, in which a street barrel-organist is making everyone happy (Bobby Harron is seen in a small part) is followed by Walthall at home reading

124

a book, which in turn is followed by a scene of his child playing alone in a park.

The theatre still plays the comedy, of people being made happy in company, and we see again the child playing alone. After the show, Blanche meets her friends and they walk off into the park. They inevitably come across the child, and Blanche embraces him passionately. Meanwhile Walthall discovers that the child is missing, and goes upstairs to find him. Blanche arrives with him, and their meeting is one mixed with embarrassment and genuine regret. Walthall eventually asks her to stay, but she declines, saying, MY WAYS ARE NOT YOUR WAYS. After many histrionics, Blanche leaves.

A short epilogue, with the title, OIL AND WATER—EACH TO ITS OWN ELEMENT features a scene of Blanche and her friends drinking champagne whilst Walthall and his family are grouped round the table listening to his reciting from a book.

Of the films already mentioned, *Gold Is Not All* and *A Drunkard's Reformation* also contain references to this particular theme.

If Griffith's moralising seems a little strained to us now, it should be remembered that Griffith had stumbled into an art still very much in its infancy, but one which had already obvious possibilities as the mouthpiece of artistic opinion to a massive audience, and it is this that Griffith recognised as its main potential. In fact, later events showed that if anything he underestimated the power of the motion picture over its audience when he made *The Birth of a Nation*. Contemporary sources indicate that Griffith was even slightly baffled over the effect that the picture had on the general public. His published response to his critics, *The Rise and Fall of Free Speech in America* attempts to defend the film on another level. He understood only then that what he had considered the faithful depiction of historical events had materialised into a dangerous incitement of racial unrest.

Griffith carried with him the desire to better the world around him. This is clear from his writings and above all from the films themselves. Invariably Griffith showed what he considered to be an ideal situation and then disrupted it with the ensuing action; or he showed this state in contrast to some less satisfactory situation, as in the case of *Gold Is Not All*.

A good example of what Griffith saw as the perfect world is to be found in a late AB made in March 1913, *Fate*. The beginning of this film is absolutely typical of Griffith's opening sequences. After the first title, which reads WHERE LOVE RULES, we see Mae Marsh playing with her pet puppy, in a small shack in the midst of a wood somewhere in the West. We also see her grandfather (Lionel Barrymore) and her small sister, asleep in a corner. A while later, her grandfather brings her home a small kitten, and there follows a short series of close-ups of the kitten and the puppy in a small basket. Griffith could never resist, it seems, resorting to animals when the scene demanded a sense of contentment and happiness. He did this on innumerable occasions, even in the features that followed his departure from Biograph.

*   *   *

During these years with the American Mutoscope and Biograph Company, David Wark Griffith made hundreds of films of incredible diversity. He made comedies, dramas, adaptations of literary classics, home-spun philosophy tales, Westerns—in fact, he explored nearly every aspect of pictorial story-telling between 1908 and 1913. Many of these films are understandably straightforward and although interesting are not particularly outstanding in view of Griffith's best work of this period. Edward Wagenknecht, in his book *The Movies in the Age of Innocence*, says,

> "If one were to judge by what many film critics have written, one would conclude that all Biograph films were a tightly woven tissue of tricky, brilliant technical devices, a never-ending show of virtuosity for its own sake. The reverse is the case. The devices are used sparingly and only when they are needed; you can look at a good deal of film without encountering so much as a single close-up. And this is just as well, for it will not do to leave the impression that Griffith was merely a technician."[40]

On the other hand, however, there remain the films—and there are a good many of them—that are undeniably masterpieces in their own right. The list seems endless; but in fact it represents only a small proportion of the total production during these four years.

The one *genre* that we have not yet fully discussed is the Western.

Mary Pickford against a backdrop of the Hudson River in THE SONG OF THE WILDWOOD FLUTE (frame enlargement)

Griffith made many, and those of them that we have been able to view suggest strongly that he held an affection for the subject, and that he found the *genre* a particularly comfortable one in which to work.

One of the earliest of these, *The Song of the Wildwood Flute* (1910) includes, as the sub-title tells us, "Authentic Indian Customs." A good deal of impressive photography, including one shot of an Indian on a hilltop in the foreground with a breath-taking vista beyond, makes it a memorable film, even though it is rather thin on the dramatic counterpoint which distinguishes Griffith's best work in this *genre*.

The following year he made another film with an Indian theme, *The Squaw's Love Story,* also known under the title *The Twilight Song.* This film has already been discussed generally for the themes within it of jealousy, revenge, and misunderstanding. A long and complicated series of events includes a fight on a high rock overhanging a river, and ends with one of the protagonists falling into the water in a spectacular dive from the top of the rock. The fight was apparently covered by three separate cameras from three different angles simultaneously. This was, if correct, certainly unique for 1911. However there is no direct evidence of this technique from simply viewing the film, and one can therefore only surmise that this course of action was taken by Griffith as a precautionary measure, and not out of any artistic considerations.

Iola's Promise (1912) is a film amongst many in which Griffith chose as his theme the white American's war with the American Indian. This picture concerns an Indian girl's affection for a gold digger who saved her life, and how, eventually, she gives her life to save the prospector's *fiancée* and her father.

A similar situation is to be found in a picture completed two years previously called *The Broken Doll,* in which a young Indian girl, given a doll by a white child, warns the settlers of an impending Indian attack and thereby prevents a massacre. She is fatally injured herself, however, and dies clutching the broken doll—a symbol, freely interpreted, of the shattered possibility of Indian/American co-existence.

There are two films of this type, and dealing with this particular aspect of American history, that stand out as exceptional works. They warrant deeper analysis and more careful attention than has been alloted to the films so far examined in this chapter. They are *The Massacre* and *The Battle at Elderbush Gulch.* Griffith had been making Westerns regularly since he began directing films at Biograph. During his first month as a director he made a picture called *The Redman and the Child*; and the titles between that date (July 28, 1908) and the release of *The Battle at Elderbush Gulch*—after Griffith's departure from Biograph—(March 28, 1914) indicate by their great number the popularity of the subject both with Griffith and his audience.

The Massacre (1912) centres around Blanche, who, after rejecting the passively amorous advances of her guardian John Bulstrode, explains to him that she is planning to marry Stephen Royston, a young soldier. Bulstrode, who is a retired officer, gives his consent, and decides to join the army once again, but this time as a scout.

The army stages a surprise attack on an Indian village, wiping

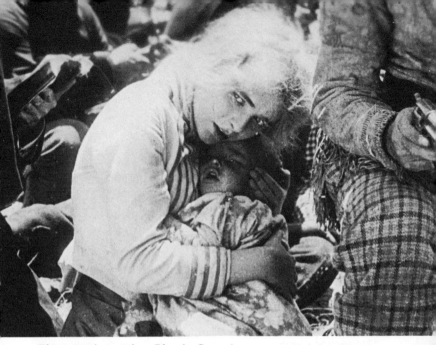

The protective mother: Blanche Sweet in
THE MASSACRE (frame enlargement)

out all but a handful of its inhabitants. The tribe's chief swears
vengeance on the white man and his people.

Meanwhile Blanche and her husband (and, by this time, their
baby) feel the urge to move West, and join a wagon train. Blanche's
husband is called away from the train on business, and, while he
is gone, the train is attacked by the revengeful Indians, who succeed
in wiping out the entire party. But a scout manages to get word to
the cavalry, who send a detachment to the train's aid. Blanche's husband hears of the attack, and rides off with the cavalry. They arrive
to find the whole scene one of complete massacre; but from beneath
the body of Bulstrode, killed while defending Blanche and her baby,

THE MASSACRE (frame enlargement)

there appears a hand . . . Blanche and her baby are safe, protected by the corpse of her former guardian.

The closing sequences of *The Massacre* demand closer study simply because of the detail and visual approach to this very simple but extremely effective narrative. Using a device which he had employed many times before in previous films, Griffith gave the film a perspective, a visual depth which distinguishes his work from that of his contemporaries. In the scenes in question, we are shown action that takes place simultaneously in the foreground as well as the background. One complements the other both dramatically and visually, giving us a sense of the geography of the scene as well as serving to economise at the same time as expanding the narrative line. The first scene where this is found comes at the end of the cavalry's gratuitous attack on the Indian village, when the chief and his surviving braves mount the hill above the village and look down on the burning remains of their homes. The chief, in the foreground with his back to the camera, swears revenge on the White man while we can plainly see the ruined village below, still smouldering, and the remains of a cavalry detachment continuing to ride back and forth in the background.

Probably the most impressive sequence in this film is one in which we see the wagon train—in extreme long shot—from the top of a hill overlooking a wide and flat plain. In the immediate foreground we see a prairie dog wander into the picture. A large bear ambles up the hillside towards the camera and frightens the dog out of the way.

The scene shifts to the wagon train itself. We see Bulstrode riding up to Blanche's wagon, thus being reminded of her vulnerability, and that of her baby, while she is without the protection of her husband.

Again, the scene returns to the hilltop, where the bear is still sniffling around the foreground, while the wagon train can still be seen in the distance. Eventually the bear moves out of the picture. Immediately we see what appears to be a second bear; but then we realise that it is in fact an Indian, disguised as a bear, spying on the wagon train below. The title, THE INDIANS SCENT THEIR PREY, follows this shot, and we are left with a precise and disturbing picture of the action that is inevitably to follow. This short sequence is so constructed as to communicate all the relevant details quickly and dramatically.

There are several other examples in this film of the "movement on two planes" idea which are worth mentioning while not being exactly akin to the two mentioned above. When the wagon train moves off into Indian territory, in one shot, the following displacement of action-within-the-frame can be recorded: two or more wagons at the beginning of the shot begin to move across the screen in the foreground from left to right, while behind them in the middle distance a line of soldiers march in the opposite direction, across the screen right to left. When the two wagons have gone out of the picture on the right, more wagons pass through the lines of soldiers, still marching across the picture, and lurch towards the camera.

Also, later in the film, the cavalry are seen racing to the besieged wagon train. In one particular shot, they ride furiously across the screen in the background from left to right, turn towards the camera just as they are about to disappear from the frame and ride towards us on the extreme right of the screen. When they reach the immediate foreground they turn abruptly out of the picture on the right.

131

The Massacre was released in November 1912. In March of the same year, a film already mentioned, *Iola's Promise,* was also released. The titles in both films have some affinities that are worth mentioning. In an almost identical situation, with an Indian attack on a wagon train, a shot of the settlers is followed by the title, LAST STAND—THE CIRCLE OF DEATH. Shots of Indians on horseback, appearing and disappearing in clouds of dust and gunsmoke, make this an extremely exciting and dramatic sequence. In the parallel sequence in *The Massacre,* a panorama of the battle from a great height follows the title, IN THE VALLEY OF DEATH. And, a little later on, preceding a shot of Bulstrode shielding Blanche and her baby, the title, THE SCOUT'S TRUST IN THE NARROWING CIRCLE.

This situation is repeated in several films. In *The Last Drop of Water* of 1911, Robert Henderson writes that "the climax of the picture was the rescue of the remnants of the caravan by the U.S. Cavalry." And the same idea can be seen in a slightly variant form in both *Fighting Blood* (1911) and the two-reel *The Battle at Elderbush Gulch,* made in the summer of 1913, released in the spring of 1914.

The story of *The Battle at Elderbush Gulch* concerns Sally (Mae Marsh) and her young sister, who are sent to visit their brothers, the Camerons. The trouble begins when the local Indian tribe celebrates their Feast of the Dogs. Sally, who has brought with her two pet puppies, is told in no uncertain terms by her brothers that the dogs are to be kept out of the cabin. She therefore puts them, in their basket, outside the door. Before she decides to bring them in for the night, they manage to escape, and, as might be predicted, two passing Indians find them. Sally is beside herself finding them gone, and is even more distressed when she sees the two Indians about to murder both of them.

One of the Camerons arrives on the scene to find Sally struggling desperately with the two Indians. He shoots one of them dead, and while Sally runs to safety with her two dogs, the remaining Indian drags off the body of his dead comrade brave. Unluckily for the Camerons, and, as it turns out, for the entire local white population, the dead Indian is the chief's son. Thus a full-scale retaliatory attack is launched, precipitating one of the most, if not *the* most exciting and impressive climaxes to be found in an AB.

The Battle at Elderbush Gulch is one of the most complex Biograph films. This is facilitated by the fact that it is in two reels, although Griffith had previously attempted similarly constructed films, with a main narrative supported by subsidiary threads of action, in several one-reel ABs (e.g. *Home Folks*). The main narrative line is that of Sally and the Camerons; but early on in the first reel we are introduced to Lillian Gish and Bobby Harron, portraying a young couple arriving at the town with their baby—and, as the title informs us, the town's first.

When the Indian attack on the town begins, Bobby has arrived for a short visit carrying the baby. Invited into the saloon for a quick drink, he gives the baby to a woman to hold. As the Indians surge through the streets, she in turn passes it to a nearby cowboy. He runs for shelter, and when Bobby runs from the saloon at the sound of gunfire, he is panic-stricken to find his baby nowhere to be seen. Just then he is struck by an Indian bullet, and staggers to the roadside before collapsing.

Meanwhile Lillian has taken refuge with the Camerons, who decide to fight it out in the cabin, Sally and her sister being confined to their sleeping-quarters.

Already therefore the sub-plot has divided itself, with Lillian at the Cameron's encircled cabin, screaming hysterically for her baby; Bobby has been wounded, although we do not know how badly; the baby itself has disappeared in the arms of a cowboy.

Into these threads is now woven another: one man has volunteered to ride to the nearest cavalry outpost with the news of the attack, and throughout the fight that follows we are constantly reminded of his perilous ride.

Incredibly all these threads are joined almost simultaneously, and quite independently of one another, although of course each is obviously dependent on the other ultimately. If the baby is not rescued, Lillian and Bobby are tragic figures and this is not Griffith's plan. If Bobby does not survive the same is true; if the help from the cavalry is not forthcoming then the whole situation is negated. How the situation is resolved, and how exactly these sub-plots are independently resolved, are shown with classic simplicity, so that the real complexity of the film is not immediately apparent, nor is that complexity ever allowed to result in incomprehensibility.

After the woman had thrust the baby into the cowboy's arms, he ran with his comrades to the Camerons' cabin, only to find it already under pressure from the Indians. They are forced to take refuge in an out-house, where they ward off the invaders as best they can. All this, of course, unknown to Lillian who sits dazed by her grief in the cabin.

Sally tries to comfort Lillian, but without success. She suddenly remembers her dogs, who are now kept outside her sleeping-quarters and are hauled in through a specially constructed hatch which she persuaded one of the Camerons to build for her. She drags them in, and puts them into the bed with her young sister.

Meanwhile the Indians succeed in firing the out-house, and the cowboys, including the one with Lillian's baby, are forced out into the open. He is soon shot and fatally wounded. A close-up shows the crying child still held in the cowboy's death-grip.

Sally, in her childish curiosity, looks out and sees by chance the baby. She immediately connects the baby with Lillian, and without telling her determines to rescue it. She first urges her sister and the dogs into an old trunk for safety, before clambering out of the dog-hatch. Risking her life, she manages to reach the baby and return to the cabin. She immediately climbs into the trunk with the child, without telling Lillian that her baby is safe.

Bobby, meanwhile, regains consciousness and stumbles out to the road. The volunteer has also succeeded in reaching the cavalry and collapses from exhaustion as the detachment mount and ride off in the direction of the town.

The Indians soon have the cabin near submission, for the Camerons have almost run out of ammunition. As the Indians are battering down the door, a close-up of Lillian shows the gun of an unseen cowboy behind her turned towards her head.

Bobby scrambles out into the path of the approaching cavalry and is picked up by one of the soldiers. They arrive at the Camerons' cabin in time to fight off the Indians and rescue the whole party within the cabin. Bobby runs in, and is greeted with joy by Lillian. The joy soon turns to distraught grief, however, when she realises that he no longer has the baby. As he tries to explain, the top of the trunk opens, and out pops Sally, her sister, the two dogs and . . . Lillian and Bobby's baby!

Thus this magnificent film ends, all is well, and even the Camerons become fond of Sally and her wretched dogs—the cause of all the trouble—now that she has redeemed herself by this heroic rescue.

The way in which this film is photographed alone makes it of prime importance in Griffith's early work. There are many extremely impressive shots, with "the entire frame filled with sweeping arcs of action." At one point a high-angle shot shows the inhabitants of the town running across a wide flat plain pursued by Indians on horseback, falling from the shots of each other's guns. There are to be found the by-now familiar high-angle shots of the cabin with Indians on horseback circling it and firing on it, seen before in *The Massacre* and *Fighting Blood*. There is a superb sense of chaos as the Indians storm the town, with women and children running to and fro among the panic-stricken cowboys, firing hopelessly at the charging Indians.

The use of parallel action is put to use here with more effect and with extraordinary dexterity than before, in part due to the film's elaborate construction. The Camerons are introduced to us parallel with Sally, Lillian and Bobby travelling to the town by stage-coach. And naturally Griffith puts this device to good use as the volunteer rides for help, cutting back and forth from him and his encounters with ambushes, to the Camerons besieged in their cabin. He also uses it in establishing Bobby in the procedure of events.

The Battle at Elderbush Gulch was made about the same time as *The Coming of Angelo* (July 1913) already discussed for its advanced command of cinematic language and complexity of construction. This only points to the truth that David Wark Griffith had, by the time that he parted company with Biograph, reached a peak in film production.

7. Comedy and Keystone

THE COMEDY FILM is as old as the cinema itself. The Lumière Brothers are credited with introducing the comic element into film in 1895 with *L'Arroseur arrosé* (*The Sprinkler Sprinkled*), first screened in America at Keith's Union Square Theatre, New York on June 29, 1896. However, on January 9, 1894, Thomas Edison had copyrighted *The Sneeze,* thirty seconds of film showing Fred Ott, younger brother of the precision room superintendent at the Edison laboratory, sneezing.

This film has an interesting history. Barnett Phillips, a regular contributor to *Harper's Weekly,* had visited the Edison plant, and was impressed by what he saw. Intending to write an article on Edison's work, he had written to the latter on October 31, 1893: "What I wanted were the illustrations of a sneeze . . . Might I then ask if you could not kindly have some nice looking young person perform a sneeze for the Kinetograph?" After some delay, Edison eventually asked his assistant W. K. L. Dickson to photograph the sneeze, and this was done on January 7, 1894. Phillips's piece appeared in *Harper's Weekly* on March 24, 1894.[17]

In France, Georges Méliès had perfected the comic trick film, and many of his productions were pirated in the States by Sigmund Lubin, who would block out the Méliès trademarks which usually appeared in some prominent position in each scene, and insert his own. Lubin's assistant at this time, Fred J. Balshofer, recalls (in *One Reel a Week*) that one day he screened a print of *A Trip to the Moon* for a customer, who suddenly leapt from his seat, and shouted, "You want me to buy that film? I made that picture. I am Georges Méliès from Paris." Lubin glared at the irate Frenchman, and then proceeded to tell him of the difficulty that Lubin had in blocking out the trademarks.

Apart from the comedy films and players mentioned in other chapters, American film comedy came into its own from 1910, the year in which **AL CHRISTIE** became director of Nestor Films. This company was part of Centaur Films, founded by David Horsley (an Englishman born in County Durham), and of which Al Christie had been general manager since 1907. The Nestor Company moved its operational base from New Jersey to California in 1911. Horsley and

Al Christie

Christie arrived in Hollywood, hoping to find a suitable building for use as a daylight studio. They chose Blondeau's Tavern and the building next door, which had once been used by the Salvation Army. Here, on October 27, 1911, they produced Hollywood's first film, *The Best Man Wins,* starring Victoria Forde. The latter appeared later for the company in many Eddie Lyons and Lee Moran comedies, and also worked for Selig playing opposite Tom Mix. She retired from films as Mrs. Tom Mix.

The choice of the name Nestor for the new company is perhaps a subtle reference to the Company's fights with the Patents Company. In Greek mythology Nestor was the wise leader who accompanied the Greeks to Troy, and returned victoriously to his own kingdom after the war. Nestor wisely left the East, centre of the Patents Company's power, and led the exodus of the independents to California.

Eddie Lyons and Lee Moran

The Company triumphed as film producers, and eventually saw the Patents Company wiped out.

The Best Man Wins was a drama, but Al Christie was soon to persuade Nestor to abandon dramas and concentrate on the production of comedy films. Nestor introduced a number of important players to the screen. *The Best Man Wins* also featured Harold Lockwood, who at the time of his death in 1918 had become one of the American cinema's most popular leading men. Eddie Lyons and Lee Moran were the company's comedy team, appearing in films with Victoria Forde as the leading lady who invariably chose Eddie Lyons. The latter also wrote and directed many of these comedies.

Betty Compson, who became a star after her performance in George Loane Tucker's 1919 production of *The Miracle Man,* entered films with Nestor in 1915. Priscilla Dean and Edith Roberts were attractive leading ladies who spent many years with Nestor. Wallace Reid worked for two years with the Company as a writer, director and actor.

Billie Rhodes, a neglected comedy talent

Sincerely, Rhod

Billie Rhodes in WHEN MARY TOOK THE COUNT (frame enlargement)

One of the most charming of early comediennes was **BILLIE RHODES**, who became "The Nestor Girl" in 1914 after making her screen *début* with the Kalem Company in 1913. Typical of her hundred or so Nestor comedies is *When Mary Took the Count*. Billie Rhodes is a young lady who does not realise how lucky she is to have Jack (Jay Belasco) as her *fiancé*. She wants a sophisticated continental for her future husband, and to this end places an advertisement in the newspaper stating "a young lady of great means and character desires to meet young man of similar qualifications." However Mary's father, Edwin Clark, and Jack plot to teach Mary a lesson. Jack disguises himself as a Count, sweeps Mary off her feet with his suave, continental manners, and eventually the couple become engaged to be married. On her wedding day Mary realises that the Count's over-politeness is a bore, and longs again for Jack. During the wedding ceremony she faints, and comes round to find that the man she is marrying is not the Count but Jack. *When Mary Took the Count* is typical of Nestor comedies; knockabouts, slapstick comedy was out, and its place taken by a polite, "genteel" form of comedy.

Billie Rhodes appeared in Nestor's first two-reel comedy, *What Could a Poor Girl Do?*, playing opposite Lee Moran in 1915. She became a feature star in 1919, appearing in Robertson-Cole's *The Blue Bonnet*. Shortly afterwards she disappeared from the screen, and now lives in retirement in North California. The few comedies of hers that are available for screening today prove her to be a comedienne equally as versatile and delightful as Mabel Normand.

"Polite" comedy was introduced to the screen by Nestor's general manager, Al Christie. As *Picturegoer* commented in 1922, "He does not seek to raise the guffaw by resorting to the grotesque or the vulgar. The secret of this merchant in screen fun is to persuade the world to laugh with his shadow characters on the silver sheet, and not to titter *at* them."[42] Christie was born in London, Ontario on November 24, 1886. He supervised all Nestor comedies. In 1915, he directed his first feature-length film, *Mrs. Plum's Pudding,* which featured Eddie Lyons, Jean Hathaway and Marie Tempest, making her only silent film appearance.

In 1916 Al Christie left Nestor and formed his own comedy producing company, releasing through Mutual. Many future stars worked with Christie, including Colleen Moore, who appeared in Christie's first feature film for his own Company, *So Long Letty* with Grace Darmond and T. Roy Barnes, released in 1919 by Robertson-Cole. In 1920 Christie's Company became part of the Educational Pictures group (with its famous trademark of the Aladdin's lamp and its slogan, "The spice of the programme"). From 1927 to 1930, Christie was independent again, releasing through Paramount. Finally in 1932 Christie rejoined Educational, with whom he remained until his retirement from the film industry in 1941. Al Christie died in Hollywood on April 14, 1951.

His contemporary, Hal Roach, said of him: "Al Christie and I were very close friends. Both Al and his brother, Charlie Christie, did very well in the comedy field, and then Al's brother got into real estate and forgot pictures. Then, I don't know what happened, but all of a sudden they went 'plunk' and lost all their money."*

* In an interview with the author.

HAL ROACH was born in Elmira, New York on January 14, 1892, and had a variety of jobs, including gold prospecting, before he arrived in Los Angeles around 1912. Purely by chance, he became an actor with the Bison Company (part of the Universal group). He soon became an assistant director, and later a director with the Essanay Company. At the same time he founded his own producing company, The Rollin Company, and began to make a series of comedies with **HAROLD LLOYD**.

Lloyd had already appeared in films for the Edison Company before he joined Hal Roach. In the first series of films they made together Lloyd played the character "Willie Work," which Roach himself admits was a "definite imitation of Chaplin." The first "Willie Work" comedy, *Just Nuts,* was described by *The New York Dramatic Mirror* as "an exaggerated slapstick comedy." In 1915, Roach and Lloyd decided on a new character for the latter to play—"Lonesome Luke." However, the comedy style was still very much an imitation of Chaplin and Sennett, with Lloyd wearing baggy pants and large comic shoes and getting involved in chases with comic policemen.

Then in 1919 came *Bumping into Broadway,* in which a new Lloyd with glasses was introduced. Here was the first indication of the Lloyd of feature films of the Twenties; the American boy who found life so full of problems. Hal Roach told me that the idea came about because "all comedy at that time was based on English comedy and I had an idea that if I made a young American and played him straight, I could do the same funny things we had been doing."

Bumping into Broadway was the first two-reeler made by Lloyd and Bebe Daniels, who had been his leading lady for several years previous. (Bebe made her screen *début* with the Kalem Company, for whom her mother was casting director.) The success of the Lloyd series, amongst others, enabled Roach to build a new studio in Culver City in 1920, and it was in the Twenties and the Thirties that Roach became Hollywood's leading purveyor of film comedy, while his only real rival, Mack Sennett, took the downward path to bankruptcy and oblivion.

Theodore Huff has written, "Sennett is rightly called the father of American film comedy. Despite some influences from early French

Harold Lloyd and Hal Roach

farce and trick pictures, his wild action, slapstick, play upon physical disaster, inspired nonsense, and burlesque of every convention and institution, sacred or otherwise, is indigenously American. But if he had contributed nothing else, Sennett would be sure of a place in history as the man who ushered Chaplin to his movie *début* and gave him his first lessons in screen comedy."[18]

MACK SENNETT was born Michael Sinnott in Richmond, Canada, on January 17, 1880, the son of Irish immigrants. He apparently wanted to become an opera singer, and he told of his desire to Marie Dressler, and she gave him a letter of introduction to David Belasco. Sennett, however, entered the world of entertainment on his own initiative, not as an opera singer, but as a vaudeville entertainer.

Like so many of his actor and actress contemporaries, Sennett learnt of the easy money to be made by appearing in films, and in 1908 he was hired by Wallace "Pop" McCutcheon, the head of the Biograph studios. Sennett was to remain with Biograph for the next four years, and to rise from bit player to director; his success is not all that surprising considering that his mentor at Biograph was D. W. Griffith. Sennett has said, "So far as any knowledge of motion picture technique goes, I learned all I ever learned by standing around and watching people who knew how."[14]

In 1909, he appeared in perhaps his first slapstick comedy (he had already appeared in over twenty films), *The Curtain Pole,* directed by D. W. Griffith. *The New York Dramatic Mirror*'s reviewer picked one part of the film out for particular comment: "We have a chase carried out with plausible consistency and fairly seething with surprises and laughable collisions and situations." The chase was, of course, to play a very important part in Sennett's later Keystone comedies. Sennett's role in *The Curtain Pole* was that of an excitable Frenchman who tries to help his friends hang a curtain on a curtain pole, and it was perhaps this role that made Sennett realise that most of all out of life he wanted to make people laugh.

In 1911 the Biograph Company were in California when the second unit's director, Frank Powell, became ill. Sennett asked, and was allowed, to take his place. In the same year he directed his first comedy, *Comrades,* with Del Henderson, Vivian Prescott, Grace Hen-

Mack Sennett, "The King of Comedy"

144

derson and Sennett himself. Typical of Sennett's comedies of this period is *Snookie's Flirtation,* which stars Ford Sterling (one of the original Keystone Kops) as a layabout who takes a position in a shoe shop in order to flirt with the female customers. When his wife discovers him so occupied, the shoe shop becomes a battle ground, filled with flying footwear.

1911 also saw the first film directed by Sennett and starring Mabel Normand. The film was *The Diving Girl,* released on August 23; the picture also featured a group of bathing girls. **MABEL NORMAND**

Mabel Normand "as beautiful as a spring morning"

was not only a brilliant comedienne, she was also a very fine actress and a very beautiful girl; Sennett describes her as being "as beautiful as a spring morning."[8] Mabel, like Sennett, built her acting career on a strong foundation, working for several years under D. W. Griffith. She was born in Boston on November 16, 1894, and moved with her family to New York in 1908. Mabel came to work for Biograph, and appeared in an unknown number of one-reelers. Incidentally, at this time Biograph did not identify their players, but so popular were they that the English distributors, M. P. Sales, gave their own names to the players. Mabel became Muriel Fortescue, just as Blanche Sweet was known as Daphne Wayne, Mack Sennett as Walter Terry and Mary Pickford as Dorothy Nicholson.

Mabel left Biograph for a short period to work for Vitagraph, but she soon returned to her old company, until she left with Sennett in 1912. She remained with Sennett for many years, and at one time they were reported to be considering marriage, but apparently Mabel became jealous of Sennett's affection for Mae Busch and called the marriage off. In 1916 Sennett formed the Mabel Normand Feature Film Company, and the first production of the new organisation was *Micky*. In this seven-reel feature, Mabel played a country girl, very much a tomboy, who becomes mixed up in society. The hero was played by Wheeler Oakman, and the villain was Lew Cody, who was to play an important part in the last years of Mabel Normand's life. *Micky,* for an unknown reason, was not released until 1918, but when it was eventually shown it proved to be a tremendous success. But by this time Mabel had left Sennett and become a Goldwyn star.

Then on February 1, 1922 the English-born director, William Desmond Taylor, was murdered. Mabel Normand was one of the last people to have seen him alive. Although she was not at any time suspected of the crime, Mabel became the victim of cheap newspaper rumour and innuendo; there was much talk of her being a drug addict. The public turned against Mabel and her films. She returned to Sennett to star in features such as *Oh Mabel Behave* and *The Extra Girl,* but they were not successful. Finally, in 1926, Mabel starred in three two-reel comedies in Hal Roach's "All Star Series," *Raggedy Rose, One Hour Married* and *The Nickel Hopper.*

According to Colleen Moore, Mabel became lost and disillusioned. She married Lew Cody, whom she had known since childhood, in

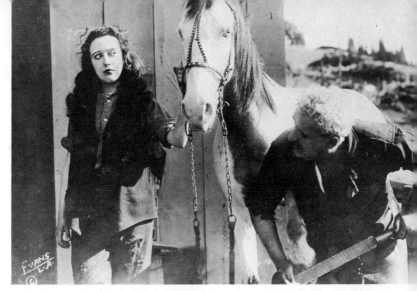

*Left: Fatty Arbuckle and Mabel Normand
in HE DID AND HE DIDN'T*

Above: Mabel Normand in MICKY

her quest for security and friendship. In 1930 she became ill with tuberculosis; she died on February 2, 1930 at the age of thirty-five.

At the time of her death, Mabel Normand was very much a victim of the Hollywood that she was partly responsible for creating; a Hollywood that did not exist when Sennett severed his connection with the Biograph Company in 1912. According to Sennett, "One day I got into the accountancy department. Griffith films were getting the acclaim but the Mack Sennett films were making more profit for the studios."[14]

Sennett was approached by Charles O. Bauman and Adam Kessel, who had formed the Bison 101 Company, and subsequently lost all rights to the use of the name in a legal tangle with Carl Laemmle. The Keystone Company was formed in January 1912; its trademark was adapted from the Pennsylvania railroad. Sennett officially joined Keystone in the summer of 1912. The first advertisement for the new Company in the trade papers read: "Keystone films. A quartet of popular fun makers, Mack Sennett, Mabel Normand Fred Mace, Ford Sterling, supported by an all-star company in split-reel comedies. A Keystone every Monday. First release September 23: *Cohen Collects a Debt* and *The Water Nymph,* featuring Mabel Normand, the beautiful diving venus. Amusing subjects cleverly acted by world famous actors."

Cohen Collects a Debt was not well received by the critics. *The New York Dramatic Mirror* reviewer wrote: "As one sits through this eight or ten minutes of senseless, idiotic horseplay he wonders what it is all about. Never once is the spectator allowed to grasp the thread of the story, if there is a thread, and all he is treated to is a continuous show of waving arms and prancing feet." This reviewer, however, has hit on the secret of Sennett's films. They lacked any sort of logic; there was no legitimate reason for whatever happened on the screen. The pace at which the comedy was put over was the most important thing, and this pace was maintained by the use of skilful editing, editing techniques that Sennett had learnt from Griffith at Biograph.

By 1913, the Keystone company of players was beginning to take shape. Roscoe "Fatty" Arbuckle left Selig to come and work for Sennett, and here also was Arbuckle's wife, Minta Durfee. Chester Conklin, who had worked as a circus clown, joined Keystone, as did Frank Hayes, who so often played the Sennett "old lady." Wallace MacDonald began his film career with Keystone in 1913, and later became a fine dramatic actor, often playing opposite Mary Miles Minter. Charlie Chase, who was to rise to screen prominence as a comedian in his own right in the Twenties, was one of the Keystone stock company in 1913.

Other players to join Keystone at a later date were Syd Chaplin (brother of Charlie), who appeared in a number of Sennett comedies, including *Giddy, Gay and Ticklish, Fatty's Wine Party* and *Gussle the Golfer.* His last Keystone was Sennett's second feature-length comedy, *The Submarine,* produced in 1916. Non-comedy players who worked at Keystone included Owen Moore, Juanita Hansen, who appeared with Ford Sterling in *His Pride and Shame,* and Douglas

Fairbanks, who appeared in the 1916 Keystone, *The Mystery of the Leaping Fish*.

Raymond Hitchcock entered films with Sennett in 1915. Hitchcock, popularly known as "Hitch" or "Hitchy-Coo", was one of America's most famous stage comedians—he introduced the song, "All Dressed Up, And No Place to Go." In 1916 Wallace Beery, with his wife Gloria Swanson, left Essanay to join Keystone. Beery had starred in a number of Essanay comedies as a female impersonator.

Chaplin came to Sennett's Edendale Studios (described by Gene Fowler as "the citadel of slapstick"[7]) in February 1914, and remained with Sennett until December of the same year, when he left to join Essanay (*see* Chapter Four). While at the Keystone studios, Chaplin graduated from a walk-on part in his first film, *Making a Living,* to become director, scriptwriter and star of his last Keystone comedies.

Making a Living, and particularly Chaplin's part in the film, was not to Sennett's liking; Chaplin found it difficult to work in the frenzied Keystone style, and he did not as yet understand the technique of film-making. However, both Sennett and Chaplin persevered, and in Chaplin's next film, *Kid Auto Races at Venice,* Chaplin's immortal tramp was introduced for the first time. According to Theodore Huff: "Chaplin was told to go in a funny costume. He put one together from what he saw around him—oversize pants belonging to Arbuckle, size 14 shoes belonging to Ford Sterling (each placed on the wrong foot so they would stay on Chaplin's small feet), a tight-fitting coat, a derby that was a size too small (belonging to Minta Durfee's father), a bamboo cane, and the small toothbrush mustache (cut down from one of Mack Swain's)."[18]

Chaplin appeared in a new comedy every week, making thirty-five in all for Sennett. Of these, all but the first twelve were written and directed by Chaplin. The most famous of all of Chaplin's Keystone films is the six-reel feature, *Tillie's Punctured Romance,* released on November 14, 1914, and directed by Mack Sennett. Chaplin is a city slicker, who attempts to steal an inheritance from "little," naïve country girl, Marie Dressler; Mabel Normand is Chaplin's partner in crime. The film's climax is a fantastic chase with the Keystone Kops, Marie Dressler *et al* finishing up in the ocean.

In 1915 Sennett's contract with Kessel and Bauman came to an end, and he took his Company to the newly-formed Triangle Film

Naïve country girl Marie Dressler with city slicker
Chaplin in TILLIE'S PUNCTURED ROMANCE

Corporation. Harry Aitken resigned from the Mutual releasing organisation, as did Griffith (with his Reliance-Majestic Productions) and Thomas Ince (with his KayBee Productions). Thus Triangle was formed with three distinct production companies, those of Griffith, Ince and Sennett. Triangle's slogan was, "Triangle is the sign that says—Come In." Aitken announced that "Triangle would take the greatest stars of the stage in their greatest plays and translate them to the screen in productions that would establish new standards."

In the years that followed, Mack Sennett prospered. New stars, such as Louise Fazenda, Harry Langdon, Marie Prevost and Phyllis

Haver, arrived at the studios. In 1917, Sennett gained absolute control of his company, and began releasing through Paramount. In 1922, he summed up the reasons for the success of his comedies: "There are two characters on the screen that the audience feel vicious toward. These are the policemen and the man in the top hat. For some extraordinary reason, they feel abused if you let a man in a top hat escape unscathed. They want something done to him. I imagine the reason for this is something deeper that the mere fact that a top hat looks funny falling off. After all, the joke of life is the fall of dignity. And the top hat is the final symbol of dignity."[28]

The coming of sound, coupled with the Wall Street crash in 1929, were partially responsible for Sennett's downfall (Sennett is said to have lost $5,000,000 on the stock exchange). Slapstick comedy could not make an easy transition into sound. In 1933 Sennett filed a petition in voluntary bankruptcy.

Mack Sennett in the later years of his life "directing" Abbott and Costello

Sennett's contemporary, Hal Roach, was quite dogmatic about his opinion of the reason for Sennett's downfall. "Sennett would put nobody under contract. He said this is the Mack Sennett Studio; I'm Mack Sennett. If they don't want to work for me, I'll get somebody else, and they'll be stars. If Sennett had put the people under contract look who he'd have had. He would have had Chaplin, Arbuckle, Al St. John, Ford Sterling and so on, they were all his people. Mack was a very rough character. He didn't want anybody running his business, he didn't want anybody under contract."*

Mack Sennett died on November 4, 1960. The films that he made over fifty years ago have become popular again, and they make vast sums of money for the people who bought the rights in them from Sennett when he was down-and-out. They are shown in truncated, badly duped versions on television sets all over the world; perhaps it is for the best that Sennett is dead and cannot see what they have done to his films.

Sennett's legacy is not his films, but the directors who have carried on the Sennett comedy tradition; Mal St. Clair, René Clair, Frank Capra and Preston Sturges all owe a great deal to Mack Sennett.

* * *

Two small comedy companies, releasing through Universal, who were specialists in one-reel comedies were Joker and L-KO.

Joker produced only one-reel knockabout farces. Gale Henry was its leading lady, and she was usually partnered by Max Asher. In a typical Joker comedy, *When Schultz Led the Orchestra,* Gale Henry is the wife of music hall violinist, Schultz, who pays more attention to the ladies of the chorus than to his wife. Needless to say, when Gale discovers this, there is a stand-up fight that surpasses anything even Sennett would have considered acceptable. The content of other Gale Henry one-reelers can be guessed from titles such as *Phyllis Falters* and *Mines and Matrimony.*

L-KO's leading lady was Alice Howell, who had first entered show business in musical comedy in 1907. In 1914 she joined Sennett, and became famous as the Keystone "scrub lady" with her fuzzy hair and penguin walk. She left Sennett and joined L-KO in 1915, and became one of the screen's finest eccentric comediennes. It is obvious that had she been given better material than was provided her by

* In a recorded interview with the author.

154

Alice Howell in A MERE MAN'S LOVE (frame enlargement)

L-KO, she would have become quite a big star. One of my favourite Alice Howell comedies is *A Mere Man's Love.* The plot is too confused and complicated to be related here—L-KO managed to cram into two reels what any other company could not have put into a six-reel feature. Suffice it to say that it is a parody of high melodrama with Oliver Hardy as the villain. Alice is a simple country maiden who gets mixed up with high society; in one uproarious scene she uses the long trains on the dresses of the society ladies to convey her from one room to the next. The film, I believe, was also the first to use the gag of the girl about to steal a pie when she sees the stern warning on the wall, "Thou Shalt Not Steal." However, she decides to commit the crime when on the other wall she sees the motto, "The Lord Helps Those Who Help Themselves." (The same gag was later used by Mary Pickford in *Rebecca of Sunnybrook Farm.*) Other popular Alice Howell comedies were *Lizzie's Lingering Love* (with Phil Dunham) and *Alice in Society* (with Joe Moore).

L-KO's two leading directors were William Worthington and John G. Blystone. The latter later became a competent director in the Twenties and Thirties; his credits include the sound version of *Tol'able David* and Laurel and Hardy's *Swiss Miss*.

All L-KO comedies were under the general supervision of Henry (Harry) Lehrman. Lehrman emigrated from Austria to the U.S.A. in 1908, and began his screen career with American Biograph. He later joined Mack Sennett in 1912, where he soon acquired an immensely valuable knowledge of the rudiments of screen comedy as one of the original Keystone Kops. He left Sennett in 1914 and became head of production for both L-KO and Sterling Comedies. He remained with these two companies until 1917, when he left to found Fox Sunshine Comedies (L-KO went out of existence in 1918 when it became Century Comedies).

Lehrman's Sunshine Comedies were of the type that featured lions and scared Negroes. After the success of Hal Roach's *Our Gang* series, he produced a series for Fox, titled *The Fox Sunshine Kiddies*. Among the players in Fox Sunshine Comedies, all of whom Lehrman brought with him from L-KO, were Billie Ritchie, Eva Novak (sister of Jane), Reggie Morris and Billy Armstrong. After the demise of Sunshine Comedies, Lehrman remained with Fox, working in the script department there, until his death at the age of sixty in November 1946.

Finally, a brief mention of a few of the early comedy features and their players. At Vitagraph, Cissy Fitzgerald appeared in some of the earliest comedy features between 1914 and 1915 with titles such as *How Cissy Made Good*. Also at Vitagraph the following year, Lillian "Dimples" Walker appeared in a series of comedy dramas.

John Barrymore began his film career as a light comedian in films for Famous Players-Paramount. Other popular Paramount comedy feature stars were Marguerite Clark, "the four foot ten fairy," in the *Babs* series, Victor Moore in the *Chimmie Fadden* comedies and Vivian Martin; all leading comedy stars between 1916 and 1920. One of the greatest of female impersonators, Julian Eltinge, was the star of a series of Paramount-Artcraft comedy features during 1917 and 1918. Over at the Fox studios, the leading comedy star was Smiling George Walsh. Between 1916 and 1918, Mutual released a series of comedies featuring Marguerite Fisher as "Miss Jackie of the Navy."

8. Pearl White and the Serial Queens

THE SERIAL FILM was one of the most popular *genres* offered to filmgoers before and during the First World War. Even today, when one discusses the early American cinema it is Pearl White or—more strangely—Grace Cunard who are remembered with the greatest pleasure.

It was no chance that brought about the introduction of the serial or series films. The film companies were quick to realise that the fans would return week after week to see their favourite stars—the quality of the production mattered little. The press also had much to do with the introduction of the serial. Newspaper owners saw that if they were to serialise a story in their journals at the same time as the films were being screened, their circulation figures would rise. Filmgoers would want to read about the stories as well as see them.

Series of films with the same leading characters were nothing new in Great Britain. As early as 1909, the Clarendon Company of Croydon had been releasing one-reelers featuring "Lieut. Rose R.N." fighting his way through a series of adventures, while British and Colonial Films of Finchley offered Percy Moran and Dorothy Foster in the "Lieutenant Daring" series. From France came the "Nat Pinkerton, Detective" series and "Nick Winter" (based on the fictional Nick Carter). Urban in France even produced a Western series featuring "Arizona Bill." And of course there were the fantastically popular "Fantomas" serials of Louis Feuillade.

It was the Edison Company that released America's first serial in 1912. It was titled *What Happened to Mary?* and starred Mary Fuller. The serial was released in collaboration with *The Ladies World,* publishers of the story. Six one-reel episodes, each complete in themselves, were released at the rate of one a month. The first episode was titled *The Escape from Bondage,* and was written by Bannister Merwin. In Great Britain, the story was serialised in *Home Chat.*

What Happened to Mary? was a tremendous success and made a star of Mary Fuller. It was followed by a sequel, *Who Will Marry Mary?* also written by Bannister Merwin in six separate episodes. In the first chapter, *A Proposal from the Duke,* Mary was involved with an impoverished duke, played by Ben Wilson. The Edison Company's publicity commented: "As Mary is now a millionairess, it is natural to suppose that she will be sought after by men of various stages and ages—the duke is the first—but you must not miss any of the others!"

The first true serial with episodes ending "to be continued next week" was Selig's *The Adventures of Kathlyn,* released on December 29, 1913, in association with the Chicago *Tribune.* Each two-reel episode was adapted by Gilson Willets from the story by Harold MacGrath, and directed by Francis J. Grandon. The star of the serial was Kathlyn Williams, "the girl without fear," and week after week she escaped death from lions, tigers and other animals provided by

Kathlyn Williams

*The villainous Marguerite Snow escapes for yet another
episode of THE MILLION DOLLAR MYSTERY*

the Selig zoo. Miss Williams was born in Butte, Montana, and had
had an extensive stage career before she entered films with the Selig
Company. She retired from the screen as Mrs. Charles Eyton, the
wife of a Hollywood producer, and died aged sixty-five on September
23, 1960.

The Adventures of Kathlyn established the popularity of the serial
film, and companies rushed into further productions. Eager for a successor to *Who Will Marry Mary?* Edison released *Dolly of the Dailies,*
again with Mary Fuller and directed by Walter Edwin. Mutual released
Our Mutual Girl, a fifty-two episode serial—each chapter one reel in
length—which told of a simple country girl who was to finish up fifty-

two weeks later as a wealthy society lady. Norma Phillips was "The Mutual Girl."

Pleased with the financial success of *The Adventures of Kathlyn,* and the subsequent increase in its circulation, the Chicago *Tribune* embarked on a further serial, *The Million Dollar Mystery,* produced by the Thanhouser Company. Twenty-three episodes long, the serial ran concurrently to the film version in the *Tribune* in the States, and in *Reynolds News* in Great Britain. The plot, written by Harold MacGrath and Lloyd Lonegan, told of a secret society called "The Black Hundred," and its activities in trying to gain control of a lost million dollars. There was a kidnapped heiress, played by Florence La Badie, a villainous countess played by Marguerite Snow, and a handsome, heroic newspaper reporter essayed by James Cruze. In the first chapter, the players were introduced and the audience told of the parts that they were playing, rather similar to a modern film trailer. Then, in the final chapter, the entire cast was brought back again, linked hands and said farewell, as a curtain descended upon which was written "Goodbye" in orange blossom.

The Million Dollar Mystery was said to have cost $125,000 to produce, and brought in $1,500,000 for its backers. A sequel was obviously demanded.

The Chicago *Tribune* conducted a scenario contest, with the winner receiving a cash prize of $10,000 for the best serial story. The winner was Roy L. McCardell, the only professional writer to compete in the contest; his story was titled *The Diamond from the Sky,* and it was produced by the American Flying A Company at its Santa Barbara studios. (Kalton C. Lahue in *Continued Next Week* claims that the serial was written by Terry Ramsaye, who at that time was the editor of the *Tribune.* However low newspaper editors may stoop, it is doubtful that they could stoop this low.) "Emphatically the greatest film ever produced, a ceaseless cataract of action—The Serial Wonderful!" claimed the studio publicity concerning this story of the diamond heirloom of the Stanley family. Thirty two-reel episodes told of the endeavours of the villains, William Russell and Charlotte Burton, to secure the heirloom from Irving Cummings and the gipsy heroine, Lottie Pickford (sister of Mary). The serial, which was released on May 3, 1915, was directed by Jacques Jaccard and William Dean Tanner. The latter subsequently used the name of William Desmond

Taylor, whose murder in 1921 was to bring about the termination of the film careers of Mary Miles Minter and Mabel Normand.

The Kalem Company entered the serial field in 1914 with a series of two-reel dramas featuring Alice Joyce. Concurrently as each episode was released in Great Britain, the story was published in *Home Notes*.

The same year saw the release of the most famous of all Kalem serials, *The Hazards of Helen,* produced from 1914 to 1916 in 119 episodes. The series was the brainchild of J. P. McGowan, who, apart from directing many of the episodes, also played the villain of the piece. Later episodes were directed by Paul Hurst, Leo D. Maloney, Robert Vignola and James Davis. The original Helen was portrayed by **HELEN HOLMES**. Miss Holmes started her screen career with the Keystone Company in 1912; her first film being *King's Court,* starring Mabel Normand. The latter was later to introduce Helen to J. P. McGowan. McGowan was so impressed by a scenario entitled *The Girl at the*

Charlotte Burton, Irving Cummings and Lottie Pickford in THE DIAMOND FROM THE SKY

ARTHUR'S CHOICE.

Helen Homes in THE HAZARDS OF HELEN

Switch, written by Miss Holmes, that he decided to film it with **Helen** in the leading role. From this one-reel drama the idea of the *Hazards of Helen* serial was to develop. Shooting took place at Glendale on the outskirts of Los Angeles.

Miss Holmes and McGowan were later to marry, but they were subsequently divorced, and Helen married Lloyd Saunders, a film cowboy and stuntman. She died of a heart attack in July 1950; her last film being the 1938 Western, *Beyond the Law.*

Australian born, John P. McGowan had made his screen *début* with the Kalem Company, his previous careers had included a boundary rider' in the Australian outback and a dispatch rider during the Boer War. He acted in and directed innumerable Kalem productions before his departure in June 1915. He appeared in many films, usually Westerns, until 1938, when he made his last film appearance in *Prairie Thunder* for First National. The last years of his life, prior to his death

162

J. P. McGowan and Ruth Roland, two Kalem stalwarts

in 1952, were spent as secretary to the Screen Directors' Guild in Hollywood.

An article in a 1915 issue of *Pictures* gives some idea of the exploits that Miss Holmes indulged in: "In *Helen's Sacrifice,* she rode a horse over a fifty-foot cliff, and leapt from the saddle on to the footplate of a fast speeding locomotive. In *The Girl at the Throttle* she averted a terrible railroad disaster by driving an engine at sixty miles an hour. In *The Stolen Engine* she leapt from the footplate of one engine onto the cab of another travelling in the same direction on a parallel track. In *The Black Diamond Express* she made an exciting dash through the clouds in a monster biplane. In *The Escape on the Limited* she drove a steam railcar at breakneck speed, and in *The Girl Telegrapher's Peril* she leapt from a trestle into the river below."

In 1916, Helen Holmes left Kalem to join Signal, and so popular were the *Hazards* that it was decided to continue production with a new Helen, Helen Gibson. Miss Gibson was born, Rose Helen Wenger, in Cleveland, Ohio on August 27, 1894. Her film career was probably the longest of any Hollywood actress. She entered the film industry in 1911, playing small parts for the Bison 101 Company under the direction of Thomas Ince. Her days as a star of Western and similar films were over by the mid-Twenties, but she remained in films, playing small parts or understudying stars such as Ethel Barrymore and Marie Dressler. She eventually retired in 1960.

When either Helen Holmes or Helen Gibson were unavailable for filming due to illness or the like, their parts were quite often played by other actresses such as Anna Q. Nilsson or Elsie McLeod.

As popular as *The Hazards of Helen* was Kalem's *Girl Detective,* first released in the autumn of 1914, and featuring Ruth Roland. The series was directed by James Horne, making his *début* as a director; previously he had only worked as an assistant to George Melford. After completing eight episodes of the serial, Ruth left Kalem to join the Balboa Company, and her part in the series was taken over by Horne's wife, Cleo Ridgely.

At Balboa, **RUTH ROLAND** appeared in several serials, released by Pathe. These included *Who Pays?,* released in twelve three-reel episodes complete in themselves and with Henry King as leading man, and *The Red Circle,* with Ruth as a wealthy girl cursed with a crimson circle on the back of her hand which forced her into a life of crime.

In 1919, Ruth Roland became her own producer, making serials for release through Pathe. The first of these serials was *The Adventures of Ruth,* directed by William Parke and written by Gilson Willets. Throughout the Twenties, she made several serials, all of them very popular, and one of them (*White Eagle*) was directed by W. S. Van Dyke. She once said, "I like to think of my serials as high-class fairy tales."[12]

Ruth Roland died at the age of forty-four on September 22, 1937. She had appeared in two talkies, *Reno* and *From Nine to Nine* (produced in Canada).

In February 1915, Kalem released in the United States a series of three-reelers "showing the application of the Ten Commandments to present day conditions," produced in association with the Christian

Science movement. The autumn of 1915 saw the release of *The Virtues of Marguerite,* starring the petite Marguerite Courtot. In each episode, complete in itself, Miss Courtot outwitted one opponent or another until eventually in episode sixteen, she was allowed to marry her ever patient lover, played by Richard Purdom. The series was directed by Hamilton Smith, John E. Mackin and Robert Ellis.

Marguerite Gabrielle Courtot was born in Summit, New Jersey on August 10, 1897, and had been an artist's model before making her screen *début* in 1912. She remained with the Kalem Company for three years before signing a contract with Famous Players. About 1920 she appeared in a number of serials for Pathe.

The chief serial offering from Kalem in 1916 was *The Social Pirates,* released in fifteen episodes. The serial, written by George Howard, starred Marin Sais and Ollie Kirby as "Mona and Mary, two very attractive young women who had become embittered by the experience of some of their close friends against mankind in general, but particularly against a class of notorious men who make it their business to profit by the weakness of the opposite sex by blackmailing and other despicable methods. In fact, so embittered have the two girls become, that they register a solemn oath to devote their lives to a campaign of retribution against that class." True Boardman was the chief villain, and in support were Frank Joanasson, Thomas Lingham and Paul Hurst. James Horne was the director.

In the same year Kalem released the *Stingaree* series, based on the stories of F. W. Hornung. James Horne was again the director, and the series starred Marin Sais and True Boardman. The series was remade by RKO Radio Pictures in 1934.

Marin Sais was a popular Kalem actress, particularly in Westerns, where her skill as a horsewoman could be seen to advantage. Her husband was another popular Western star, Jack Hoxie (who also appeared in several episodes of *The Hazards of Helen*). Miss Sais made her last film appearance in *The Fighting Redhead* (1951). She was the star of one of the last Kalem serials, *The American Girl,* released in seventeen two-reel episodes. Edward Hearn was Marin Sais's leading man in this picture of Western life. On its release in Great Britain in July 1918, *The Bioscope* commented, "each episode is quite a complete sensation."

With Kalem, another important producer of serials was the Universal organisation and its associated companies. Universal's first serial offering, *Lucille Love, Girl of Mystery*, was released in fifteen episodes on April 14, 1914. As the story was unfolded on the screen, it was published in the *Chicago Herald* in the U.S.A. and in *The Weekly Dispatch* in Great Britain. "Who was Lucille, girl of mystery with the beautiful face hidden by a black mask?" demanded the publicity handouts. Apparently, "she was the daughter of a well-known officer in the army, but tiring of a life of adventure, had decided to settle down in the peaceful calm of wedded life, and was now touring the world in search of a husband." This world tour brought Lucille Love, complete with black mask, to many cinemas. It soon became very apparent that there were a large number of Lucille Loves touring the world, and that the film Lucille Love bore a striking resemblance to the Universal star, **GRACE CUNARD**. Teamed with Grace Cunard as leading man and director for this and future Universal serials was Francis Ford. (Ford's brother, John, also appeared in small parts in several of these serials.)

Miss Cunard was born, Harriet Mildred Jeffries, on April 8, 1893 in Columbus, Ohio. She made her first stage appearance at the age of thirteen, and had been touring with Eddie Foy before she entered films in 1910 with the American Biograph Company. She also worked for Lubin and Kay Bee before signing a contract with Universal. Miss Cunard and Francis Ford formed an ideal screen partnership. Apart from starring in the serials, they also wrote their own scenarios, edited and titled the productions, and quite often shared directing honours. After her serial career was ended, Grace stayed with Universal and played opposite Elmo Lincoln in the 1919 *Elmo the Mighty*. In 1920 she appeared in a series of two-reel Westerns, and continued to play small parts during the Twenties and Thirties. She even appeared in some sound serials, including Tim McCoy's *Heroes of the Flame*. She was still remembered with affection by numerous admirers at the time of her death on January 19, 1967.

The second serial from Universal, *The Trey O' Hearts*, released in fifteen episodes, was the work of writer Louis Joseph Vance and director Wilfred Lucas. Cleo Madison starred in the dual role of two identical twins, innocent Rose and villainous Judith. Clever trick photography made it difficult for the audience, as well as leading man George Larkin (who later was to star in the Kalem series, *Grant, the Police Reporter*) to tell the one from the other. Later in 1914, Universal also released

Grace Cunard and Francis Ford

The Master Key, directed by and starring Robert Z. Leonard. Ella Hall was the leading lady in this story of a lost mine. As a publicity gimmick, Universal offered serial fans the Master Key Brooch, "the fad of the hour. Snap it on your sweetheart's wrist. You wear the key that unlocks it."

The second Cunard/Ford serial, *The Broken Coin,* was released to an eager public in twenty-two episodes on June 21, 1915. It was the story of a broken coin that would, when pieced together, show a map to a lost fortune. Carl Laemmle made his first screen appearance as a newspaper proprietor, who sends out his chief reporter, none other than Grace Cunard, on the quest for the treasure. *The Broken Coin* also introduced a new serial star, Eddie Polo.

Polo was the strong, masculine hero, "the Hercules of the screen," on whom every young boy tried to model himself. His strength was legend; he was said to be able to lift three men at one time. In *The Broken Coin,* he easily caught Grace Cunard in his arms, after she had jumped 15 feet down from a balcony. He was the first man to jump from the Eiffel Tower with a parachute. In 1915, he leapt from a plane 4,280 feet in the air, and proved that parachute jumping from a plane was feasible at any height. Polo came from a circus family. He arrived in California on November 2, 1913, and eventually obtained a small part in a Billie Ritchie comedy at the L-KO studios. He later worked for the company as a stuntman, but longed to appear in films as himself. Eventually, he was introduced to Francis Ford, who hired him for a small part in a two-reeler *The Campbells Are Coming.* He stayed with Universal for eight years, and appeared in many serial including *Peg O' the Ring, The Grey Ghost, Circus King* and *Cyclone Smith.* Unfortunately, as Polo became more popular with filmgoers, he became less popular with the people that he was working with. He became conceited and pompous. He quarreled with Universal, and set up his own production company to make a serial version of *Captain Kidd* in 1922. It was not a great success; Polo died alone and destitute in Hollywood on June 15, 1961, aged eighty-six.

One of the last Cunard/Ford serials, *Peg O' the Ring* was released in fifteen episodes from May 1, 1916. Set in a circus, Grace Cunard played the title role of Peg, whose mother had been bitten by a leopard

Eddie Polo demonstrates his horsemanship to Peggy O'Dare

An English poster for THE VOICE ON THE WIRE

shortly before her daughter's birth. This mishap resulted in Peg's acquiring the unfortunate habit of scratching and tearing at anything in sight on certain nights. Miss Cunard was not very happy with the production, and at one time she walked out and her part was taken over by Ruth Stonehouse. The Grace Cunard/Francis Ford partnership ended with the release of the sixteen episode *The Purple Mask* (*The Purple Domino* in Britain) in December 1916. It has been claimed that the success of these serials was in many ways responsible for the expansion of the Universal Company.

Another popular serial partnership at the Universal studios was that of Ben Wilson and Neva Gerber. They starred in two serials in 1917, the fifteen episode *The Voice on the Wire,* directed by Stuart Paton, and *The Mystery Ship,* directed by Harry Harvey and Henry McRae. The former was concerned with "The Black Seven," a secret society with "advanced theories of life and death." *The Mystery Ship* dealt with the ever popular subject of lost treasure.

Liberty, a Daughter of the U.S.A. introduced Marie Walcamp as a Universal serial star in the summer of 1916. The twenty episode serial was set in Mexico, and Miss Walcamp portrayed, as was the heroine in so many serials, an heiress. Marie Walcamp's other major serial for Universal was *The Red Ace,* with the heroine proving her father and brother innocent of charges of treason in the wilds of Canada.

Essanay entered the serial field in January 1916 with *The Strange Case of Mary Page,* a fifteen episode crime story written by Frederick Lewis and directed by J. Charles Haydon. Edna Mayo was the heroine, with Henry B. Walthall as her lover. Each episode revolved around the evidence offered at a murder trial, with a flashback to the actual crime. From the Vitagraph Company came *The Iron Test* and *The Perils of Thunder Mountain,* both released in 1918 with Antonio Moreno and Carol Holloway.

In 1916, Billie Burke starred in *Gloria's Romance,* a twenty episode serialisation of a modern romantic novel. Described as "The Serial Supreme," it was a supreme failure. Harry Houdini entered films in 1919 with the serial *The Master Mystery.* Arthur B. Reeve was the author of this story of a robot that destroyed everything in its path, with heroines Marguerite Marsh and Ruth Stonehouse about to suffer a similar fate except for the quick intervention of Houdini.

One of the most charming of the later serial players was Irene Castle, already famous as a dancer with her husband Vernon, when she entered films with the serial, *Patria. Patria* was a beautiful young girl who thwarted enemy spies, led by Warner Oland, and saved America from invasion. Milton Sills, making his first major screen appearance, played the Secret Service agent hero. The serial was produced by William Randolph Hearst's International Films for release through Pathe. Intended as pro-war propaganda, at a time when America was still neutral, the serial was banned for a time. When the serial was eventually released, much of the war scare had died down, and the film was not a tremendous success.

The most famous of all serial stars of any country and of any time was **PEARL WHITE**, to whom the remainder of this chapter is devoted. Pearl was a very attractive actress; Joe Franklyn has said of her, "she was a lovely girl in a healthy, open-air, big sister fashion."[8] She was beloved by her fans. One wrote of her: "When I met Pearl White in Paris during 1934, of course, she had changed a tremendous amount since the early serial days, but, her original beauty was evident. It was her personality and general kindness that held her comparison in my mind to the heroine I had conjured up in the film personality of so long ago. She appeared to me to be a person of extreme honesty—straight and clear thinking. For my own point of view, after so many long years of 'fan' admiration, Pearl White realised all I had ever dreamed of. I look back on my meeting Pearl White as the finest climax one could realise. Pearl White appeared to be somewhat of an enigma . . . but, subsequently over the years, in Paris and in Cairo, I met people who were her intimate friends over many years, and their views were as mine."

Pearl Fay White was born on March 4, 1889 in the small Missouri village of Greenridge. After attending school in Springfield, Missouri, she joined a small company of touring players, and this eventually led her to obtain small film roles with the Powers Film Company of New York in 1910. The following year she joined the Lubin Company in Philadelphia, but was later fired.

After a brief period with the Pathe Company, again in New York, she became a leading comedy actress with the Crystal Film Company. She remained with Crystal until early in 1914, and her comedies were fairly popular. *Moving Picture World* said, "Pearl White has a large following among picture fans, and she deserves to have."

In 1914 Pearl returned to Pathe to begin work on the Company's first serial, *The Perils of Pauline*. Badly written and badly directed (by Louis Gasnier and Donald MacKenzie), the twenty episode serial was a sensational success. It was produced with the financial backing of William Randolph Hearst, who is said to have titled the serial, and of course gave it maximum publicity in his newspapers.

The following, taken from the original campaign book, gives some idea of what audiences in 1914 thrilled to: "Episode One. 'Twix Earth

Pearl White

Crane Wilbur warns Pearl in
THE PERILS OF PAULINE

and Sky. Stanford Marvin died leaving a huge fortune to be shared between Harry, his son, and Pauline, his ward. If, however, Pauline died within a year without marrying Harry, Raymond Owen, Marvin's secretary inherited everything. Owen set himself out to encompass Pauline's death and whilst snap-shotting her in the basket of a balloon, arranged for someone to create a panic by rushing into the crowd. Then Owen cuts the ropes. 'My God!' gasped Harry, in horror. 'The balloon has escaped, and Pauline is alone in mid-air!' " Paul Panzer was villainous Raymond Owen, while Crane Wilbur was dashing Harry.

The Perils of Pauline was followed by Pearl's greatest serial success, the thirty-six episode *The Exploits of Elaine,* directed by Louis Gasnier and George B. Seitz. The serial was also published in the Hearst newspapers in America, and in *The News of the World* in Britain.

In this adaptation from the detective stories of Arthur B. Reeve (the American Conan Doyle), Arnold Daly was Craig Kennedy, the famous detective, Creighton Hale played Jameson, his likeable young assistant, and Pearl was Elaine Dodge, in pursuit of her father's assassin,

174

and forever at the mercy of Sheldon Lewis, "The Clutching Hand." Other villains that Miss White encountered in the serial were Lionel Barrymore as Marcus del Marr and Edwin Arden as Wu Fong.

So successful was *The Exploits of Elaine* that two sequels were later released; *The New Exploits of Elaine* and *The Romance of Elaine*. There was even a popular song, still remembered today, written in praise of Elaine and her exploits:

> "Elaine, Elaine, I love you all in vain.
> Elaine, Elaine, you've set my heart aflame.
> Of all the girls you're the sweetest I've seen,
> Always to me as sweet as sweet sixteen.
> I dream of you all through the livelong day,
> And then when I see you, you fade away.
> Elaine, Elaine, please come down from the screen,
> And be my Moving Picture Queen!"

Creighton Hale warns Pearl in
THE EXPLOITS OF ELAINE

Pearl White was the Queen of the Serial Queens. The estimated audience for her serials in America alone was fifteen million. She made seven further serials, all of them immensely successful. She also starred in a number of features, not so successful, for Pathe and Fox.

In 1922, Pearl made her final serial, *Plunder,* with her old director, George B. Seitz, and for her old company, Pathe. The following year, she sailed for France, where she starred in three features, the final one being *Terror.* Pearl travelled extensively, and entertained lavishly. She had an apartment in Paris and a château at Biarritz. Pearl passed away on August 4, 1938. Undoubtedly the most popular star of the early American cinema, Pearl White never set foot in California; all of her films were made in either New York or Paris.

9. Conclusion

OF ALL THE EARLY COMPANIES that made up the Patents Group only Vitagraph survived after the First World War. The reason for the decline of these early companies is not difficult to discover; none of their owners had the vision to realise that the cinema would and could grow and become an established art form in its own right. They were incapable of understanding that the public would, and wanted to, accept a film lasting in length more than one or two reels. The creative men, the directors, technicians and players, employed by these companies may have realised that the cinema industry could produce feature-length films, but they had little or no say in the running of the companies. Terry Ramsaye recounts an apocryphal story of a conversation between Frank Marion and William Wright of the Kalem Company: "The business is going into these long pictures. They tie up a lot of money and you have to take a chance. We will keep Kalem going as long as the short picture lasts, and then we'll quit."[25]

The film industry of the future belonged very much to the new men of the industry, producers such as Adolph Zukor and Jesse L. Lasky. The former, of course, was responsible in 1912 for the American distribution of the feature-length *Queen Elizabeth,* with Sarah Bernhardt and Lou Tellegen, directed by Louis Mercanton. Zukor and Lasky, came together to form Famous Players-Lasky, and in 1914 joined forces with Morosco and Hobart Bosworth's Pallas Company to distribute their films through W. W. Hodkinson's Paramount Corporation.

The First World War assured the new American film industry of world supremacy, and at the same time wiped out the old American film industry.

One man foresaw what the future held, and that man was D. W. Griffith. It is fitting that this book should end with a study of the last film he made at American Biograph. For the next few years of the American cinema belonged definitely to D. W. Griffith.

Judith of Bethulia can only be seen as something of a watershed in Griffith's career. In it, he developed his carefully formulated techniques of cross-cutting and also showed for the first time just how strong was his flair for the epic. In strong contrast with the cross-cutting employed in *The Battle at Elderbush Gulch,* however, the techniques as applied

Sarah Bernhardt deals a death blow to the early American cinema in QUEEN ELIZABETH (LES AMOURS DE LA REINE ELIZABETH)

here give more of a visual commentary on the main narrative rather than build the suspense or contribute to the tension of the film as a whole. In *The Battle at Elderbush Gulch,* Griffith used cross-cutting to complement each thread of the picture's complex narrative; in *Judith of Bethulia,* however, he uses it in a more subtle way: when Judith falters for a moment in her unenviable task of decapitating Holofernes, we see the starving and dead of Bethulia, whose dying Judith has come to the enemy camp to liberate. After these brief scenes, we cut back to Judith, now filled with stronger resolve. In this way, Griffith introduces a new factor into his film-making, that of involving his audience not only in his characters, but also in the *conscience* of his characters.

Griffith's love of the epic subject never really found its full scope at Biograph. Only in *Judith* can be seen his true flair for handling large crowd sequences, a flair that was to come into its own in *Intolerance* especially, but that can be seen to great advantage in *The Birth of a Nation,* as well as *Orphans of the Storm* and *America,* showing how he never really lost this particular aspect of his genius throughout his active life in motion pictures.

Griffith deals another blow with JUDITH OF BETHULIA: Blanche Sweet and Kate Bruce

The battle scenes, in retrospect, have an obvious affinity to those of *Intolerance*. Here for example the same towers can be seen rolling up to the city walls, with the falling bodies and charging horsemen. But Griffith knew that showing spectacular crowd scenes did not make an exciting sequence in themselves. Interesting detail had to be seen also; a horseman picking up a wounded comrade as he gallops across the screen, a soldier having to pull away his dead companion before being able to mount the ladder against the city walls—all this was indispensible if the sequence was to have pace and excitement.

Without the resources he was able to call upon in later years, Griffith's *Judith of Bethulia* is inevitably a modest production when such comparisons are made. But this is not to suggest that the film in any way falls short of the breadth of its creator's vision nor the grandeur of its conception. It takes as its subject the story of Judith the Devout, who in order to save her city and its inhabitants feigns love for Holofernes, the leader of the great army that lays siege to Bethulia. The film inevitably caused much consternation among the management of the American Biograph Company, not only because its subject matter

179

Holofernes is infatuated with Judith's beauty: Henry B.
Walthall and Blanche Sweet in JUDITH OF BETHULIA

demanded what appeared to them to be a preposterously large budget
but also because Griffith planned and shot the film as a four-reeler.
This idea met with a decidedly hostile reception. Griffith's habit of
exceeding the standard length of two reels had been encountered before,
and had been disapproved of but tolerated. Now, in expanding his
subject to four reels, it was felt strongly that he had overstepped the
mark. Biograph released the film after Griffith's departure from the
company, only when his reputation was gaining momentum and when
the short-sighted front office of Biograph eventually understood what
a valuable asset they had possessed in D. W. Griffith. By that time it
was too late; Griffith had gone, and taken with him many of the company's stock company, names who were to become stars in later years
as a result of their training under Griffith. Biograph had lost all that

made it unique with the advent of Griffith's departure, and that stubborn refusal to allow him to broaden his canvas ushered in the slow but inevitable decline to obscurity and liquidation of the once prosperous American Biograph Company.

For all the excitement of the battle scenes, the film is really an *interior* drama, inasmuch as the majority of the action is thoughtful and deliberate, an interchange of emotions between two characters or, simpler still, the self-examination of Judith herself, coming now into a large close-up of her expressive face and now receding to reveal the luxury of the tent provided for her by the infatuated Holofernes. Even the scenes within the walls of Bethulia, with the population dying of thirst, has a definite balletic quality, and is therefore striking not so much in how the crowd is used by Griffith but more in the way it is barely used at all; and in fact the most effective scenes are those in which the crowd is *completely* static, some figures standing alone, some in groups, some sitting and others lying prostrate in the glaring light and heat of the tropical sun.

Judith of Bethulia in many ways sums up Griffith's work at Biograph. It features several of the actors and actresses who were moulded by him during this period into great names of motion picture history; Blanche Sweet, Henry B. Walthall, Mae Marsh, Robert Harron, Lillian and Dorothy Gish, Lionel Barrymore, Kate Bruce, Henry Carey, Christy W. Cabanne, Eddie Dillon and Charles Hill Mailes. But, perhaps more significantly, it demonstrates how completely Griffith was by this time in command of his medium.

Now, in 1914, he was to forge ahead and build on his own firmly constructed foundations the new art's first and most durable masterpieces *The Birth of a Nation* and *Intolerance*. Looking again at his films for Biograph, films that in certain cases have emerged unscathed from the changing fashions of some sixty years, it is not at all difficult to appreciate why the company enjoyed such prosperity during the time Griffith was in its employ. To describe the quality which distinguishes the pictures is much more difficult. Some times it is a tangible, other times simply an abstract quality. Perhaps Griffith himself, speaking after he had described talking pictures as "stilted," looked back to those halcyon days from his years of retirement and identified the constantly sought-after goal: "It is my arrogant belief," he said in 1947, "that we have lost beauty."

Select Bibliography

A PART FROM the books and magazine articles listed below, much information was taken from the files of *The Bioscope, The Cinema, The Edison Kinetogram, Moving Picture World, The New York Dramatic Mirror, Photoplay* and *Pictures and the Picturegoer*. The clippings in the collection of the late James M. Anderson, now housed in the National Film Archive, were of inestimable value. (The number given against each of these items is used in the text to identify sources.)

1 Anderson, James M. "Look Out, It's Coming," *Motion Picture Projectionist* (January/March 1954).
2 Bodeen, DeWitt. "Theda Bara," *Films in Review* (May 1968).
3 ———."Anita Stewart," *ibid* (March 1968).
4 Brockhouser, Frank. "Philadelphia Was Hollywood Before Hollywood," *Philadelphia Sunday Bulletin* (October 22, 1967).
5 Davies, Wallace E. "Pearl White," *Films in Review* (November 1959).
6 Dunham, Harold. "John Bunny," *The Silent Picture* (Winter 1968).
7 Fowler, Gene. *Father Goose*. New York: Covici-Friede, 1934.
8 Franklin, Joe. *Classics of the Silent Screen*. New York: Bramhall House, 1959.
9 Gaye, Howard. *So This Was Hollywood!* Unpublished manuscript in the possession of Mrs. Howard Gaye.
10 Gebhart, Myrtle. "The Real Ruth Roland," *Picture Play Magazine* (December 1926).
11 Geltzer, George. "Herbert Brenon," *Films in Review* (March 1955).
12 ———."Ruth Roland," *ibid* (November 1960).
13 Gessner, Robert. "Porter and the Creation of Cinematic Motion," *Journal of the Society of Cinematologists* (Vol. II, 1962).
14 Giroux, Robert, "Mack Sennett," *Films in Review* (December 1968/January 1969).
15 Henderson-Bland, Robert. *Actor-Soldier-Poet*. London: Heath Cranton Ltd., 1939.

16   Hendricks, Gordon. "A Collection of Edison Films," *Image* (no. 3, 1959).

17   ———. "A New Look at an Old Sneeze," *Film Culture* (nos. 22/23, 1961).

18   Huff, Theodore. *Charlie Chaplin.* New York: Henry Schuman Inc., 1951.

19   Jacobs, Lewis. *The Rise of the American Film: A Critical History.* New York: Harcourt, Brace and Co., 1939.

20   Lahue, Kalton C. *Continued Next Week.* Norman: University of Oklahoma Press, 1964. An annotated list of corrections to this book by George Geltzer, a copy of which is in the British Film Institute Library, is of particular value.

21   Mitchell, George. "Sidney Olcott," *Films in Review* (April 1954).

22   Niver, Kemp R. *The First Twenty Years.* Los Angeles: Locare Research Group, 1968.

23   O'Dell, Paul. "Biograph, Griffith and Fate," *The Silent Picture* (Winter 1968).

24   Pratt, George C. *Spellbound in Darkness.* Rochester: University School of Liberal and Applied Studies, 1966.

25   Ramsaye, Terry. *A Million and One Nights.* New York: Simon and Schuster Inc., 1926. Reprinted (1964) by Frank Cass and Co. (London).

26   ———. "William Fox, One of the Fighting Greats of Film Industry," *Motion Picture Herald* (May 17, 1952).

27   Sadoul, Georges. "English Influence on the Work of Edwin S. Porter," *Hollywood Quarterly* (Vol. III, no. 1).

28   Sennett, Mack. "When They Won't Laugh," *Pictures and the Picturegoer* (March 1925).

29   ———. *King of Comedy.* Garden City: Doubleday and Co. Inc., 1954.

30   Slide, Anthony. "The Colleen Bawn," *Vision* (Spring 1967).

31   ———. "From Manger to Cross," *ibid* (Summer 1967).

32   ———. "The O'Kalems," *Cinema Studies* (September 1967).

33   ———. "The Kalem Serial Queens," *The Silent Picture* (Winter 1968).

34   Smith, Albert E. and Phil A. Koury. *Two Reels and a Crank.* Garden City: Doubleday and Co. Inc., 1952.

35 Smith, Frank Leon. "Pearl White and Ruth Roland," letter in *Films in Review* (December 1960).

36 Spears, Jack. "Max Linder," *Films in Review* (May 1965).

37 ———. "Norma Talmadge," *Films in Review* (January 1967).

38 Turconi, Davide. *Mack Sennett*. Rome: Edizioni dell'Ateneo, 1961.

39 Universal Supplement. *The Cinema* (February 8, 1952).

40 Wagenknecht, Edward. *The Movies in the Age of Innocence*. Norman: University of Oklahoma Press, 1962.

41 anon. "In the Far West," *The Bioscope* (February 9, 1911).

42 anon. "Ten Years of Jesting," *Pictures and the Picturegoer* (January 1922).

Index

(to films of the period and personalities; major film references in bold type)

189

190